THINGS
WE ALL

HAVE IN
COMMON

PETE JACKSON

10 Publishing
a division of **10** of those.com

Copyright © 2022 by Pete Jackson

First published in Great Britain in 2022

British Library Cataloguing in Publication Data
A record for this book is available from the British Library

ISBN: 978-1-914966-16-3

Designed and typeset by Pete Barnsley (CreativeHoot.com)

Printed in the UK

10Publishing, a division of 10ofthose.com
Unit C, Tomlinson Road, Leyland, PR25 2DY, England

Email: info@10ofthose.com
Website: www.10ofthose.com

3 5 7 10 8 6 4 2

For Ben, Rosie, and Sam, I love you so much. By grace, may each of you know the love of God as your heavenly Father – He's the best! – and also the joy, peace, and freedom of having the most important things in common with Jesus.

And for my church family, St Andrew's Kendray, thank you for having me as one of your pastors. May this little book help us all to share the great news of Jesus in our community and town. And may all glory be to Him.

Not to us, LORD, not to us
but to your name be the glory,
because of your love and faithfulness.
(Psalm 115:1)

ACKNOWLEDGEMENTS

Thank you to my dear friends – Jonny Parker, Penny Atkinson, Paul Parker, and Paul Williams – who kindly read and helpfully commented on the manuscript. And also to my best friend, my wife, Sharon: you are a precious gift from God, and I am so very blessed to be your husband. Thanks for all your love, support, encouragement, and partnership. In the words of Darryl Kerrigan, 'Love you, Darl!'

As a church pastor, I regularly use ideas, phrases, and illustrations from things I have read in books, blogs, and newspapers; from conversations I have had; and from sermons or lectures I have heard – ideas which have remained lodged in my head. I have tried to reference these in the notes, but am aware that I haven't a clue where some things originated! I gladly acknowledge my general indebtedness, and sincerely apologise if you should have had a reference.

CONTENTS

INTRODUCTION

I hate coffee. I believe I've only drunk it twice. The first time was as a child, when I thought it was so disgusting that I spewed it back into the mug and privately vowed never to let it pass my lips again. On the second occasion it was poured into my mouth by a well-meaning friend when I was 'going down' with hypothermia. I am grateful. Tea would have been better.

Although I hate coffee, coffee shops are okay. I can't stand the drink, but I do quite like the smell, so coffee shops are quite pleasant places. They also sell cake.

Strange as it may seem, this little book was conceived – and even partially birthed – in a coffee shop of all places. Much of it was written in a branch of Starbucks while waiting for my kids. And a few of the chapters were delivered as short talks over three evenings in Costa Coffee as part of a week of events for a church in Sheffield.

The idea was to give some food for thought, provoke discussion, and help people to consider different aspects of what we might call 'the human condition' – things that are common to us all. Then we pondered how Jesus Christ directly addresses what we are like.

Now I appreciate that most people will not hate coffee as I do – that's fine. We're all different. We live in a world in which our differences are often highlighted: our different colours, religions, cultures, sexualities, genders, abilities, ideologies, philosophies, skills, musical tastes, economic means, sporting preferences, dietary choices, and political persuasions. And there's something very wonderful about our diversity! The world would be a dull place if we were all the same.

But alongside much diversity, there are still many things that we all have in common. Some are obvious. We all breathe! We all need water, food, and shelter to survive. We all have good days and bad days. We all like to laugh and smile. We are all relational and want to be loved. We are all afraid – of something at least. We are all physical. We are all emotional. I could go on. It's fair to say that we have more in common than not.

This little book highlights some of those similarities. Each of the first twelve short chapters seeks to uncover something of what we are all really like. The book then ends with an invitation that is open to us all.

You may want to start with one of the chapters that you already know is true of you – perhaps the one on anxiety, dependency, fear, or shame? Or you may be intrigued to find out how you are a refugee or a lawyer or a worshipper? Start where you like. You could read the chapter on your own, or you may find it helpful to agree with a Christian friend to both read the same chapter (perhaps a different one each week) and then meet to discuss it. At the end of each chapter are three or four questions that might prompt thought or discussion.

Of course, so few pages could not provide a comprehensive answer to any aspect of the human condition. Nor do they attempt to do that. The aim is that they are a starting point – and a signpost to the One who does have the answers, and who actually claims to be the answer.

I hope the short chapters that follow will help you to begin to consider Jesus Christ – and to see from the Bible how, in the twenty-first century, Jesus continues to be deeply and personally relevant to each and every one of us.

Feel free to read the book with a cup of coffee. Or tea.

1

THE DESIRE
IN US ALL

I had just missed my connection and the next train would not arrive for about an hour. I decided to kill some time looking round the shopping centre by the station.

But I never made it to the shops. I got distracted en route by a fascinating exhibition of about fifty life-size photographs of random people. The pictures were mounted high on the walls around the escalator. At the top of the escalator there were more portraits of all kinds of people: black and white; young and old; people who appeared to be well off and those who were clearly poorer.

And underneath each portrait were a few words from that person. They all began with the words, 'I want ...'

Well, I couldn't resist. I spent the next forty-five minutes wandering around, looking at every single portrait and reading what each one of those people wanted. Interestingly, they generally all wanted something quite similar: life – either a happier life or an easier life or a richer life. Many of them just wanted life – that's it. They wanted to live and not die.

One person, obviously aware of how time seems to speed up as you get older, said, 'I want time to slow down.' They were expressing a desire for more life, not really wanting theirs to finish.

Another said, 'I want to live life to the end.'

Still another declared, 'I want to live life to the full.'

Someone else stated, 'I want a cure for cancer.' I imagine many would echo that deep desire for an end to diseases like cancer that cut life short.

A similar idea was evident in the next: 'I want everyone to be happy and no more war.' War not only ends lives but makes life miserable for those who survive. We want life and happiness.

A different person said, 'I want Bowie back.' I reckon we'd all love someone back. Death robs us of the people that we love and precious relationships.

One person simply wrote, 'I want more time.' And there I was, trying to kill time!

The irony was not lost on me. As I wandered around, I knew that I didn't really want to kill time at all. I, too, wished it would slow down.

Time is strange like that. On the one hand, I wanted time to pass quickly, so I could get on the train and get home. Yet, on the other hand, I am very conscious that time is zooming by all too quickly.

Turning fifty was sobering. It almost certainly means that my life is well over halfway through. As a few friends with whom I grew up also turned fifty, I decided to send them each a birthday card. I'm not usually great at that, but fifty felt significant. With each one, I couldn't help but wonder where the last thirty-five years have gone since our carefree teenage years. Time has flown! And there's something a little disconcerting about that. The passing of time points to the passing of life.

But, as the exhibition reminded me, we human beings essentially want to live. *Generally*, we don't want to die.

I have met lots of people in terrible situations, but very few who actually want to die. And even for those few, it's only because the alternative seems to be so bleak or painful that they imagine that even death would be better than continuing to live.

This common desire to live is why some people give up smoking or drink a bit less. Others take regular exercise, and even eat salad.

It's also why dying people tend to cling on. They battle for a few more days, hours, or minutes. The desire for life within them is huge and strong.

And that desire is in us all.

This is no surprise, though, because the Bible says that God has made us for life – eternal life, no less:

God has ... set eternity in the human heart (Ecclesiastes 3:11).

That's why we want to live. The desire for life is hardwired in us all. We were designed that way – with eternity in our hearts.

A mug is a simple but clever thing. It doesn't leak so it can hold liquid. It has a handle so that we can comfortably hold a hot drink without burning ourselves. And when we've finished, the mug can be washed up and used for another drink. Genius! Everything about the design of a mug tells us it would be a great thing from which to consume a hot drink.

In the same way, you and I were designed for life – God set eternity in our hearts. And everything about us, from our first cry to our final breath, is about life. Our constant appetite to grow and learn and experience and try and love and thrive is all a striving to squeeze every last bit of juice out of life – and to not die. That's why we don't like death – or what causes it.

Many regard death as an enemy. We don't even want to talk about it. So we use phrases that refer to death without actually saying someone has died: 'kicked the bucket', 'passed away', 'popped their clogs', 'kicked their oxygen habit', 'flatlined', or 'checked out'. While some are amusing, their purpose is to hide how unamusing death really is.

We don't like death, we don't want it, and we don't talk about it. And yet death is one of the few things in life that is certain. It's the ultimate statistic: one out of one dies. There are no exceptions.

Even so, we don't know much about death – except that we're all in the queue. Although we don't know exactly where in the queue we are!

But what if we could be certain of life? What if we could have the kind of life that we really crave? What if death were not an invincible enemy?

Christians believe and trust in Jesus partly because He is the one person in all history to have taken on death and won. He died on a Roman cross – His execution is well documented. But so too is His resurrection. Jesus rose from the dead and was seen to be alive by crowds of people[1] – and individuals who were prepared to stake their own lives on this fact. They saw Him; they heard Him; they touched Him.[2]

This is why Christians have hope in the face of death. Our hope is not mere wishful thinking. It is solidly based on the historical, physical resurrection of Jesus Christ from the dead.

---

1   1 Corinthians 15:6.
2   Acts 1:3; 1 Corinthians 15:3–7; 1 John 1:1–3.

Underneath all those portraits I saw were various expressions of desire – the desire for life ... or a better life ... or more life. Some of the words spoke of painful situations – such as a battle with cancer. Others expressed deep longings or a sense of being lost. The risen Lord Jesus speaks into them all:

I am the way and the truth and the life. No one comes to the Father except through me (John 14:6).

Jesus is declaring, 'I am the way' for people who are lost; 'I am the way' for those who are desperate and don't know which way to turn. If we want direction, we need Jesus. He is the way to a right relationship with God, and the only way through death.

'I am ... the truth,' Jesus continues, for people who are confused and don't know who or what to believe. Experience tells us that we can't totally trust anyone – even those closest to us can let us down. But Jesus is *the* truth: He is the one person who can be totally relied on – and especially in the face of death.

'I am … the life': Jesus has the answer to death – and He proved it by rising from the dead.

That's why Jesus is able to take us through death and give us the life that we crave – the good, full, loving, joyful, eternal life that God has hardwired into our hearts. So the Bible can confidently assure us that:

Whoever believes in the Son [Jesus] has eternal life (John 3:36).

Notice that we are all mentioned in the first word of that verse: 'Whoever …' You, me, anyone – whoever will believe in Jesus will have eternal life.

In all of this, Jesus is unique. No one else is the way, the truth, and the life. No one else is able to offer us eternal life. Only Jesus has risen from the dead, so only He can give us hope in the face of death, and only He can give us the full life that we all crave and desire. That's why Jesus also says, 'No one comes to the Father except through me.'

If you have ever noticed that desire for life in you, if you want more life … life to the full … eternal life, then Jesus is your man.

Killing time is a bad idea. It runs contrary to what we really want and for what we were really made. We all want to live. We desire life. Eternal life. Jesus says he can give it to us!

QUESTIONS TO THINK ABOUT OR DISCUSS

1. What do I want? How would I finish a sentence that begins with the words, 'I want …'?

2. Am I aware of a personal desire for life? If so, how do I express it? It may be in something positive – embracing certain aspects of life. Or perhaps it is in something that feels negative – anxiety about health or fear of death. Quite possibly it is in both.

3. What do I think of Jesus' claim to be 'the way and the truth and the life'? Am I prepared to investigate this claim?

2

THE IMAGE
IN US ALL

I used to be a graphic designer. Think of colouring in for grown-ups. One aspect of design is to portray the right kind of image – which will largely depend on what the brand or product is, and who it is aimed at.

Take Starbucks or Costa. They each present a particular image through their branding. But what if their branding used grey bubble writing? It would portray a very different image, and we'd think about them differently.

Sports brands like Adidas or Nike always have healthy, fit, talented sports stars in their ads –

because they want to portray an image that they hope lots of us will want to buy into.

But image is not only important for business. Whether we do it consciously or not, we all want to portray a particular image – even if it's that we don't care about our image!

Think about how you present yourself on Facebook. Your profile picture, the pictures you share, and the comments you make all help to project the image that you want for yourself.

Each year I make a family calendar filled with photos from the last twelve months. Looking at it, you'd think we were the perfect family. Every picture is full of smiling, happy faces. There are no pictures of me being grumpy with my wife or yelling at the kids or them having a sulk. My family calendar projects a lovely, though not entirely accurate, image.

Or consider your clothes, hair, car, gadgets, hobbies, vocabulary, accent, and musical tastes. These all contribute to the image that we personally portray to the world around us. And in many ways, we're all fabulously different!

But did you know that, essentially, we are all made in the same image? And that our image is not so much for us to reveal to the world, but is revealed to us by God?

The Bible says:

So God created mankind in his own image, in the image of God he created them; male and female he created them (Genesis 1:27).

All of us – men and women – are created in God's image.

Don't worry, that doesn't mean that we're all the same. But it is actually really great that we're all made in God's image because people made in the same image can relate to one another in a meaningful way. You and I can relate to fellow human beings – even complete strangers – in a way that we cannot relate to our dog or cat or goldfish. Being made in the same image makes it possible for us to have deep, meaningful friendships. Our pets are made in a different image. Disney, Pixar, and Aardman may brilliantly personify them, but they are animals. They are not people made in God's image. And so although we can communicate some basic things to our pets, and they to us, we don't have the same kind of meaningful relationship with them that we have with one another.

There's something else about being made in God's image that's worth knowing. It means that we are all extraordinarily valuable – regardless of our identity, status, ability, or circumstances.

We are often very shallow and foolish in our thinking, valuing people according to how clever, rich, important, talented, successful, or beautiful they are. We look at their home, clothes, qualifications, job, or hairstyle, and we make value judgements. Sadly, we write off some people. We conclude that they are not worth very much – not worth talking to; not worth bothering with; not worth helping.

But being made in God's image means that we *are* all intrinsically valuable. And, deep down, we know it. That's why, at great expense and risk, we don't think twice about sending rescue teams up mountains or out to sea to rescue anyone who is lost – regardless of how clever or important or beautiful they are. We seek to save lives regardless of nationality, gender, sexuality, age, or religion. We instinctively recognise the value of human life.

Being made in God's image means one final truth: we all reflect what God is like. As we observe other people, we often see something of God's character and goodness. For example, when someone sees that you are about to leave your phone on the train and hands it back to you, they are reflecting God's honesty and kindness. When we see a parent gently correcting their child, they are reflecting God's patience and grace. When we see a friend caring for an elderly neighbour, or someone buying a drink and food for a homeless person, they are reflecting God's care and compassion. When a person speaks up for what is right or defends someone who is being abused, they are reflecting God's love of truth and justice. Every day we will see in each other little reflections of the image of God.

But, of course, that's not the whole story. Sadly, we also see in one another what God is *not* like. Although we were made to reflect God's image, we are like a mirror that is smeared with grease and broken – and so the image of God in us is marred and distorted.

The person who was honest about your phone might use his own phone to lie to his boss about being sick because he just wants a day off work –

reflecting the slippery relationship with the truth that we all have. The person who was patient and gracious with their child might fiddle their taxes or ignore the speed limit – reflecting the rejection of authority that is in each one of us. And the person who cared for their neighbour might slag off a close colleague in an attempt to improve their own chances for promotion – reflecting the duplicity and selfishness that taints us all.

Yes, we are all made in God's image and we all reflect His image, but it's a broken and distorted image of Him that we present.

And here's the thing: because God's image in us is messed up, we don't relate to Him (or one another for that matter) in the way that He designed. He made us in His image so that we could have a meaningful relationship with Him. That is a staggeringly wonderful thought – we were made to be in relationship with the Creator of the entire universe! But our relationship with God is broken. And that leaves us feeling empty – because the very thing we were made for is not happening.

We then start to flap around trying all sorts of things in an attempt to find fulfilment, peace, contentment, and purpose. We look for a new image or identity in fashion, gender, sexuality, employment, ideology, philosophy, politics, friendships, family, sport, and so on. But none of them ultimately deliver.

Of course they won't satisfy us. We were made for relationship with God, and without that relationship we will never have the ultimate fulfilment and peace for which we long.

Wonderfully, though, the Bible tells us how our relationship with God can be restored. Because God made us in His own image, He was able to come into the world as one of us – while still being fully God. He did exactly that in the person of Jesus, His Son. The Bible says:

The Son is the image of the invisible God
(Colossians 1:15).

When Jesus came into the world, He perfectly revealed God's image in human form: He only ever reflected God's goodness and love and faithfulness and kindness. He was never selfish or unfaithful or rude or unloving. He never lied or cheated. He lived the perfect human life, but He also did amazing miracles that only God could do.

More than that, Jesus came into the world to fix us. He came to make it possible for our broken relationship with God, and for His marred image in us, to be beautifully restored. This restoration was made possible by Jesus Himself being broken and marred in death.

A few verses later in the Bible, we're told:

Once you were alienated from God and were enemies in your minds because of your evil behaviour. But now he has reconciled you by Christ's physical body through death *to present you holy in his sight, without blemish and free from accusation (Colossians 1:21–22, my emphasis).*

As He died on a cross, Jesus would have looked terrible. There you would have seen an image of shame (as He died the death of a criminal); humiliation (as He hung there naked); weakness (as He succumbed to nails being driven through His wrists and feet); and a truly horrific amount of blood and gore. It would have been the kind of image from which you would want to quickly look away. But, as the Bible states, He died this death to make it possible for people like us to be brought back to God. He was punished for our 'evil behaviour' – for all the ways we express our rejection of God. He took our punishment so that we may be forgiven by God ('free from accusation') and be presented completely clean ('without blemish') before God.

Through Jesus, we can be forgiven and reconciled to God and enjoy that relationship with Him for which we were all made. That's how much God loves us. He let His precious Son suffer and die so that we may come back to Him and live life as it's meant to be – in relationship with Him. But God doesn't leave our restoration there. He gradually and patiently renews His image in us:

> But now you must also rid yourselves of all such things as these: anger, rage, malice, slander, and filthy language from your lips. Do not lie to each other, since you have taken off your old self with its practices and have put on the new self, which is being renewed in knowledge in the image of its Creator (Colossians 3:8–10, my emphasis).

As we come back to God and receive His love and forgiveness through Jesus, our true image is renewed and restored – a restoration that will finally be complete on the day when Jesus returns.[3]

We were designed and created in God's image so that we may have a meaningful and loving relationship with Him. Being designed in God's image gives us immense value. This is seen supremely in God sending His precious Son to die so that we may come back to Him and rightly reflect His image – the image in which we were all made!

QUESTIONS TO THINK ABOUT OR DISCUSS

1. How would I say that I reflect being made in God's image?

2. Are there ways in which I know that I clearly don't reflect God's image?

---

3 1 John 3:2.

3. The Bible says that Jesus is the perfect image of God. What do I think about Jesus?

4. Being made in God's image means we are all geared up for relationship with Him. Is that a relationship I would like to explore having?

3

THE ANXIETY IN US ALL

I have never had cancer. As far as I know, I still don't. But on several occasions I have wondered. To be honest, I have more than just wondered; I have worried.

Scientists say that one in two of us will get cancer.[4] In my little family, there are five of us. I'm the one who has eaten the most lard. I'm the one who, until recently, never used sun block. I'm the one who grew up in a smoke-filled house. So

---

4   https://www.bbc.co.uk/news/health-31096218 (article dated 4 February 2015).

in my family, genetics apart, chances are I'm in pole position.

I haven't always worried about getting cancer. It all started shortly after my forty-first birthday.

A year earlier, I had received a letter from the local medical practice inviting me for a check-up – apparently standard procedure for the over forties. A check-up? Me? I laughed as I screwed up the letter and threw it in the bin.

Within a year, I had a persistent headache (which lasted over a year), tremors in my hands (which meant that I struggled to hold a book), shooting chest pains, breathlessness, and a few other symptoms that are best not written about.

The doctor sent me for various tests. Thankfully, they all came back clear or negative.

My wife lovingly jokes that I've beaten cancer about sixteen times in ten years! It always helps to laugh.

The slightly more helpful professional diagnosis was that each symptom was a physical response to stress. That's an entirely different issue.

But here's the thing: every time a different symptom appeared, I felt anxious. Really anxious.

Anxiety is, arguably, the most common psychological issue of our time. It is that inner feeling of apprehension or worry or dread.

So what was I anxious about? Well, something was clearly wrong. And I knew the stats – one in two. I also knew quite a few relatively young people whose unpleasant symptoms turned out to be bad news. Just the thought of it made me anxious.

Anxiety often spikes when we feel afraid, under pressure, or insecure. In essence, we will all feel anxious when something we love or consider important is threatened.

My various symptoms had made me wonder if my life was under threat. And, as we saw in chapter one, we all desire life – not death.

But it's not just a threat to our health (real or imagined) that makes us anxious. Anxiety rears its head when we perceive a threat to all sorts of things: our control; our reputation; our home or possessions; our job or financial security; our values; our relationships; our lifestyle.

Thankfully, the Bible has a lot to say about anxiety. It often recounts the lives of people who were clearly anxious. As you might expect, there are words of comfort.

But the first way in which the Bible helps us is by revealing the real cause for our worry. In short, life without God is an anxiety-inducing life.

When you think about it, the reason for that is obvious. Without God, we like to imagine that we are in control of our lives and circumstances. It's that kind of thinking that was (and is) part of my problem. But there is so much that we are clearly not in control of – and never can be. We can't control the weather – so our wedding or holiday could be a washout. We can't control the traffic – so we could be late for an important appointment. We can't control our ageing – so our hair will fall out or go grey, whether we like it or not. We can't control how our kids will turn out. We can't control what other people will do or say or think of us. We personally can't control how the economy will perform, or the emergence of a contagious virus.

Any one of these things could impact us in a very bad way. We lack real control over our lives. No wonder we get anxious!

When God spoke to His people through Moses, He showed them that a life lived in relationship with Him would bring blessing. But then He warned them that a life lived without Him would bring anxiety:

> ... *the* LORD *will give you an anxious mind, eyes weary with longing, and a despairing heart. You will live in constant suspense, filled with dread both night and day, never sure of your life (Deuteronomy 28:65–66).*

The point is this: when we try to live life without God, we will be fearful and anxious because we are not in control. We have zero control over many aspects of our lives. And as we get older, we become increasingly aware that, despite our best efforts, we are ultimately in control of very little. Frankly, we do not have a clue what is coming up the track even in the next week, let alone the next year or decade. Sooner or later those feelings of dread and anxiety will come upon us all.

What, then, should anxious people do? The Bible urges us to trust in the Lord – the One who really is in control.

One anxious man who depended on God wrote these words:

Unless the LORD had given me help,
  I would have soon dwelt in the silence
  of death.
When I said, 'My foot is slipping,'
  your unfailing love, LORD, supported me.
When anxiety was great within me,
your consolation brought me joy.
(Psalm 94:17–19)

Although God did not immediately remove the anxiety, He brought consolation in it. The man was aware of God's love and support – which enabled him to carry on, and even to have an inner joy.

Getting this perspective – in which God is big and powerful (much bigger and more powerful than 'little old' us), but also personal – is a huge help in dealing with our anxiety.

The Lord's Prayer is the most famous Christian prayer. It begins with the words: 'Our Father in heaven'. God is in heaven. As God, He rules over all. He's powerful. And yet He is also personal, and we are invited to call Him 'Father'. We can cry out to Him when we are anxious or afraid. It is a huge blessing to see that God, not us, is in control of the world and our lives!

God doesn't promise to take away the bad stuff in our lives, but He does promise we will never be in a situation that is not under His good and absolute control.[5] He also promises to be with those who trust Him in it – and, ultimately, to bring them through it.[6] Being aware of God's Fatherly love and goodness, but also His power and rule, is what sustains me when I am anxious.

Furthermore, through Jesus Christ, God invites us all to come to Him, to know Him, and to have Him as our supremely powerful Father – the One who really is in control! Knowing God is not a one-shot vaccine that makes us immune to anxiety. But being able to approach Him each day with ongoing, dependent trust will calm our fears and reassure us that, ultimately, we are safe. God loves us. He rules over all. And as our Father, He watches over us.

Jesus said to all who trust God as Father:

> *Therefore I tell you, do not worry about your life, what you will eat or drink; or about your body, what you will wear. Is not life more*

---

5   Psalm 73:26; Romans 8:28.

6   Psalm 71:19–20.

than food, and the body more important than clothes? Look at the birds of the air; they do not sow or reap or store away in barns, and yet your heavenly Father feeds them. Are you not much more valuable than they? ...

But seek first his kingdom and his righteousness, and all these things will be given to you as well (Matthew 6: 25–26, 33).

We typically seek first our own 'kingdom' – our own comfort, our own happiness, our own ease of life. We may seek first our physical health or material possessions or a special relationship or a particular role. And we become anxious when those things are threatened – which they all will be at some point.

But when we seek first God's kingdom, we can rest assured that, whatever happens, we are in safe hands.

The King of God's kingdom is Jesus. He is the 'Christ' – which means God's eternal King. By His resurrection from the grave, He even showed Himself to be King over death.

Living an anxiety-inducing life without God results in death. And death is anxiety-producing all on its very own! In many ways, death is the ultimate threat – it spoils and ruins everything.

But we can come to know and trust the One who has beaten death and who promises eternal life beyond the grave to all who will believe in Him. When we do that, there is hope and peace – even in the face of a life-ending disease.

The Bible urges us:

> *Humble yourselves, therefore, under God's mighty hand, that he may lift you up in due time. Cast all your anxiety on him because he cares for you (1 Peter 5:6–7).*

While we continue to pretend that we can be in control, anxiety will – sooner or later – be a major issue. We need to humbly recognise that we are not God – that we are not in control. Instead, we should come to Jesus for relationship with God – the One who really is in control. When we do that, we will know His loving Fatherly care and have assurance that we are truly safe. Only then will we start to relax. Just what the doctor ordered!

QUESTIONS TO THINK ABOUT OR DISCUSS

1. What makes me anxious? What do I worry about?

2. Who or what do I believe is in control of my life?

3. What stops me from trusting God, who is really in control and who cares for me?

4. Am I ready to humble myself before God and to cast my anxieties on Him?

4

THE ADDICT
IN US ALL

They were so young. Too young. Some were in their thirties; others only in their twenties. One of the worst things about being a church pastor is sitting with grieving parents and planning the funeral of their precious son or daughter. Very sadly, I've done it too many times. It is utterly, *utterly* wretched.

They were all addicts – typically addicted to recreational drugs or alcohol, and often both. It's so ironic that we talk of 'recreational drugs' because they don't recreate anything. They only destroy. They destroy lives; they destroy families; they destroy hopes and dreams; they destroy communities.

A friend of mine – not much older than me (and who has kindly given me permission to write this) – has been addicted to alcohol since he was a teenager, and to various illegal drugs for over twenty-five years. He used to have a reputation for being a 'hard man', and lived life in the fast lane. Booze and drugs were part of that.

Today he is a broken man. He can barely do anything. He can't walk far and his speech is often heavily slurred. Every day is a battle – a physical battle simply to live, and a constant battle with addiction. His life is still controlled by blue tins of lager and drugs that destroy. When we meet, he often weeps as he reflects on his life. He sometimes wonders about coming with me when I visit younger guys so that they can see what drugs and alcohol will do to them.

But young people probably wouldn't believe that. You see, drugs and alcohol seem to tell a different, more attractive story. Initially, they appear to promise so much – that's why my friend was drawn in.

They promise fun. They promise status and reputation. They promise satisfaction. They promise respect. They promise escape. They are lying.

In truth, they don't give anything. They are actually thieves. They rob people of everything: their money; their relationships – including their family; their health; and, finally, their life. Another wretched funeral to plan.

For those of us who have never had a problem with drugs or alcohol, it's easy to look down on drug and alcohol addicts and to think that we are better in some way. But we're mistaken. The main difference between a drug addict and me is not that I'm any better; nor that I grew up in a different environment with different influences. I'm just addicted to different things.

All of us are easily addicted – even if we don't realise it. Have you ever felt compelled to habitually consume, watch, receive, or do something? Would you feel some level of angst, upset, anger, or trauma if you were to cease doing so? That's addiction.

Addiction is a form of slavery. Even good and legal things can enslave us.

We could be addicted to what we consume: alcohol, drugs, crisps, chocolate, coffee, or even carrot juice![7]

We could be addicted to what we watch: sport, the news, pornography, or a soap opera.

We could be addicted to what we receive: love, approval, praise, or attention.

We could be addicted to what we do: shopping, smoking, having sex, working, training, biking, or gaming.

Many addictions are considered far more respectable and acceptable than an addiction to drugs, alcohol, tobacco, gambling, or pornography. But they are destructive addictions nonetheless.

Some of us are 'shopaholics'. We get a 'high' from buying new things. But the high is soon gone, and so we hit the shops again for another 'fix'.

Others of us are addicted to work – we might even refer to ourselves as 'workaholics'. On the surface this appears to be a reasonably noble

---

7 In 1974 the *New York Times* reported that Basil Brown of Croydon (in the UK) died of cirrhosis of the liver brought on by carrot juice addiction: https://www.nytimes.com/1974/02/17/archives/carrotjuice-addiction-cited-in-britons-death.html (article dated 17 February 1974).

addiction. But there is nothing noble about driving ourselves to an early grave or burning ourselves out to get to the top – and neglecting our family in the process. Addiction to work is destructive.

Likewise, being addicted to keeping fit might be regarded as admirable. But it's destructive when exercise becomes such an obsession that our life revolves immovably around a training regime to the detriment of other things, or when it causes us to never be satisfied with our weight or body shape.

Research by psychiatrists at King's College London has shown that almost a quarter of young people are addicted to their smartphones.[8] Their symptoms are certainly consistent with addiction. They can't control the amount of time they spend on their phone, using it so much that it is detrimental to other activities. They become 'panicky' or 'upset' if they are denied constant access.[9]

Other people are addicted to television, smoking, or overeating. Many are addicted to the approval of others. And it's probably fair to

---

8   https://www.bbc.co.uk/news/education-50593971 (article dated 29 November 2019).

9   Ibid.

say that we're all addicted to our own comfort, ease, and pleasure.

Of course, not everyone will be addicted in the same way or to the same degree. Some alcoholics will be constantly drinking throughout the day. Others will just need to drink each night when they get home from work or after they've put the kids to bed. Others will binge at the weekend. We are not equally addicted, but we are all addicts.

We often get addicted because we are stressed or depressed or bored. We are broken people. And, sadly, we go to the wrong place or the wrong person or the wrong thing to get fixed. We seek release, comfort, or escape by drinking or shopping or injecting or gaming or eating. Those things become our 'turn-to' thing that we hope will help us to cope.

And often they do! When we are low or stressed, a change of environment or activity is undoubtedly a good thing. But when we come to depend on those things, an addiction is formed without really dealing with whatever is actually broken.

It's as if we are thirsty and gasping for a drink, but we keep drinking seawater.[10] It's liquid. It looks like it will do what we desperately want it to do – to quench our thirst. But it doesn't. Saltwater only increases our thirst – and if we carried on drinking it, it would eventually make us ill and kill us.

Very tragically, drug and alcohol addictions do kill many people each year. It is true that an addiction to training, shopping, porn, gaming, or work is probably not going to end like that. However, nor will our addiction ultimately satisfy us – which is why we keep going back for more!

I quite like outdoor kit. If I need a new item, I research it thoroughly. I go to website after website after website looking at what is available and reading all the blurb and reviews. Lots of reviews! My wife will eventually say, 'How much more do you need to know?' The truth is I could read that stuff all day. I know I have to stop, but even as I get to the point of realising that, I find myself thinking, 'Just one more site.' You see,

---

10 This analogy comes from Steve Hoppe, *Sipping Saltwater* (The Good Book Company, 2017).

I'm not satisfied with what I've already seen and read. I want more!

Have you ever felt like that about something? Addiction causes us to always want more. One more game of Fortnite or FIFA. One more pair of shoes or bit of kit. One more beer or glass of wine. One more promotion or accolade. One more bag of crisps or bar of chocolate. One more click, one more smoke, one more level, one more one-night stand, one more go. Just one more.

But it's rarely 'just one'. Even if we stop for now, invariably we'll be back – because even the good things that we are addicted to do not deeply satisfy us. Ultimately, like saltwater, they are unsatisfying.

Listen, though, to the words of Jesus:

... whoever drinks the water I give them will never thirst. Indeed, the water I give them will become in them a spring of water welling up to eternal life (John 4:14).

Let anyone who is thirsty come to me and drink (John 7:37).

Jesus satisfies. He truly quenches our thirst.

Without Him, we are like people living in a desert – a spiritual desert. We desperately look for water – something that will give us that thirst-quenching satisfaction. We desperately look for life.

However, shopping, gaming, food, alcohol, television – or whatever your thing is – won't satisfy us and can't solve our problems. They just temporarily cover them or help us to forget them or distract us from them. And very often they enslave us in the process.

We might only realise how enslaved we are when we try to escape or to stop. That often feels impossible.

But Jesus is able to set us free. He quenches our thirst for meaning, purpose, identity, and joy. Most of all, He quenches our thirst – our desire – for eternal life. That is why He urges us to come to Him and drink.

Wonderfully, God specialises in making beautiful things out of broken things. He really does recreate people in the way they are meant to be. While drugs, and our other addictions, are not recreational – they can't recreate us – God can. Through Jesus, God sets us free from our slavery so that we may live life to the full as His children and enjoy Him forever. That is real recreation.

Jesus once told a parable (a story with a hidden meaning) in which He depicted Himself as a strong man who could release people from captivity.[11] He is in the business of setting people free so that they may have freedom from all that once enslaved them.

Therefore the apostle Paul wrote:

It is for freedom that Christ has set us free (Galatians 5:1).

Jesus sets us free from the need to be approved of or loved by others, because His love is so much better. He sets us free from having to be in control, because He really is in control. He sets us free from whatever we watch, consume, receive, or do, because He Himself and what He offers is so much better than all that stuff put together.

If you feel shackled by some kind of addiction, take heart: freedom is available. Really. The way

---

11 Mark 3:23–27.

to freedom is to come to Jesus, and for our heart to be captivated by Him – to see and believe that what He has done and won for us is far, far better than *whatever* enslaves us.

And as we trust Him, Jesus will lovingly, gently, and patiently release us, recreating us into the people we were designed to be.

QUESTIONS TO THINK ABOUT OR DISCUSS

1. What (good or bad) things might I be addicted to?

2. What do they do for me (whether positive or negative)?

3. Do I want to be free from my addiction or slavery? If so, am I prepared to consider Jesus as the One who is able to set me free?

5

THE REFUGEE
IN US ALL

It is currently estimated that over eighty-two million people in the world have been forcibly displaced from their homes.[12] They are refugees. That is a vast number of people – well over the entire current population of the UK.

Just imagine what it is like to be a refugee. You are struggling to provide for your family, living in fear, and don't know if you will survive. Even if you do, you have the prospect

---

12 United Nations High Commissioner for Refugees (UNHCR) website (article dated 18 June 2021).

of many years – perhaps a lifetime – of hardship and poverty.

What happened to drive someone from their home in the first place? There may be a number of reasons, but surely top of the pile is conflict. Terrible forms of conflict – war, terrorism, slavery, and persecution – have created millions upon millions of refugees.

And what do refugees want and need? The answer is obvious: refuge. They want somewhere safe to call 'home' – somewhere safe to live and work; somewhere safe where they can have access to food, water, and medical care; somewhere not just to survive, but to thrive.

Sadly, the situation we see in the world today is nothing new. The Bible is full of refugees. The people of Israel fled from cruel captivity in Egypt and wandered around for forty years waiting to be given a place of refuge. Shortly after Jesus was born, He Himself became a refugee because a jealous, despotic dictator wanted to kill Him. He regarded Jesus as a threat to his rule – and so Jesus' family had to flee.

Now I know this might sound strange, but there is a sense in which the Bible regards us *all* as refugees. While we wouldn't use that word to describe ourselves, many of us feel it quite acutely. We feel lost – or perhaps unsure of where life is really heading or its purpose. So we are constantly searching for somewhere to feel safe and secure and at home. Ever felt like that yourself?

Even if we feel safe and settled, the Bible's perspective is that our home is very temporary. We might have made the best of it, but, in refugee terms, we have just found a nice spot under a tree and arranged our plastic sheeting well. Regardless of how good we have made our home, we are still refugees.

And, like all refugees, we too are refugees as a result of conflict. But there is a difference. The difference is that we have caused the conflict ourselves.

Just like that king who regarded Jesus as a threat to his rule, we all regard God as a threat to our own self-rule. And so there is conflict. Often the conflict is quiet: we simply ignore God. We reject His right (as God) to rule over us. We quietly get on with our lives – living in His world and enjoying all that He has made – while seeking, as far as we are able, to live independently of Him.

That's why God rarely features in our lives – except, perhaps, when we're desperate. The rest of the time we don't even think about God, let alone talk about Him. And in one respect this is completely understandable. If we *were* to discover that God really is there, and that *He* is God and so *He* must be in charge, we would grasp that *we* can't be. Very often we don't even want to consider that possibility. We are like children who turn their back on their parents and run away from home – as if to say, 'I will live my life my way; I'm in charge!'

So we wander away from God. And we wander through life living as we please – seeking happiness, security, belonging, and refuge. In short, we want home.

In our imagination a good home consists of a safe place with people whom we love and who will love us, and some possessions that we will gradually accumulate. We find a place to live. But however nice it may be, it doesn't take long for us to imagine it's not quite the home we want. If we had the time, energy, or money, we would improve it. An extra room would be nice, or a slightly bigger (or smaller) garden, or a new kitchen, or just some redecoration.

We do something similar with our ambitions or goals, which can also be part of our searching for our place – our home – in the world. We pursue a particular goal hoping we'll find worth, value, status, riches, reputation, and satisfaction through it. But once it's accomplished, we almost immediately ask, 'What next?' or 'Where next?' And so life becomes a constant cycle of goal-setting, achieving (or failing) said goal, and then setting our sights on the next thing.

Perhaps we imagine that a spouse or family will fulfil us. But we quickly discover that being a husband or wife or a parent can be hard.

Or we buy things that we think will make us happy and content. But having enjoyed them for five minutes, a new model comes out and it's easy to suddenly feel dissatisfied with what we have – the shine has quickly worn off.

Places, people, and possessions are good – really good! But they are not home. They cannot give us permanent refuge, contentment, and safety. We become aware of how fleeting they are. Relationships break down and life can unravel; or a loved one dies and leaves us on our own. We try to insure our place and possessions against loss or damage, yet are increasingly aware of our limited capacity to keep and protect what we have.

For many, life becomes a constant striving and grasping for the right place, the right relationships, or the next thing. But we are grasping at mist.

The Bible says we are constantly striving because we are a long way from God. We are living in conflict with the One who is the source of true peace, contentment, rest, love, and refuge. So what are we to do?

Israel's most famous king – King David – once wrote these words:

> *Taste and see that the Lord is good;*
> > *blessed is the one who takes refuge in him.*
> *(Psalm 34:8)*

We're used to tasting things to see if we like them. Obviously we do this with food, but we do it with other things too. I once had the opportunity to go skiing. At first, I wasn't sure whether to go, but I decided that it was a chance to find out what it was like. I now love skiing. I wouldn't have known without giving it a taste.

The Bible encourages us all to 'taste and see that the LORD is good'. It describes those who take refuge in God as 'blessed'. A few verses later we're given a warning:

> ... *no one who takes refuge in him [the LORD]*
> *will be condemned.*
> *(Psalm 34:22)*

Those words reveal our need to take refuge in God, or we'll be condemned. God will justly condemn us for living in His world, enjoying His good gifts, and yet choosing to live in conflict with Him.

Notice, however, that no one is too far away, too bad, or too beyond the pale to take refuge. *No one* who takes refuge in God will be condemned. He loves us. He longs for us to come home and enjoy the many blessings of being in His family.

God calls us to come home and to find refuge through His Son, Jesus Christ, who said:

> *Come to me, all you who are weary and*
> *burdened, and I will give you rest*
> *(Matthew 11:28).*

Life is messy. Sometimes the mess is a result of our ignoring God. Sometimes life just stinks. Hard things come our way – financial struggles and the fear of loss; relationship disasters and the fear of loneliness; illness and the fear of death. The burdens of life are many. They weary us.

And then there's the 'baggage' we all carry – pain and hurt from the past with which we struggle to deal. What or who can be our refuge in all of these things?

Jesus is the refuge where there is real rest. Rest from all the striving and grasping; rest from our burdens. Jesus urges us to come to Him so we can join God's family – a family in which there is love, peace, forgiveness, acceptance, and ultimate safety – forever!

Without Jesus, we will remain as refugees – a long way from God and a long way from home. For some there will be constant and growing nagging: 'There must be more to life than this. I have so much, so why am I still not happy or why do I have no peace?' For others there will be a blind and naive pressing on – presuming that you're heading in the right direction or that things will eventually get better. But, all the while, you are moving further away from God.

Refugees need refuge. Through Jesus Christ, God lovingly invites you to come home to Him and to be eternally safe. 'Taste and see that the LORD is good; blessed is the one who takes refuge in him … no one who takes refuge in him will be condemned.'

QUESTIONS TO THINK ABOUT OR DISCUSS

1. Can I see how I live in conflict with God – a conflict that is of my own making?

2. When life is hard, where (whether positive or negative) do I run to for refuge?

3. Am I prepared to 'taste and see that the LORD is good'?

6

THE DELUSION
IN US ALL

Whether you liked him or not, his words certainly jarred. Tweeting on his decision to withdraw American troops from Syria, President Donald Trump told the world that he had used his 'great and unmatched wisdom'.[13]

Are you serious? Who honestly talks or writes like that? It sounds like a pantomime villain. It's the kind of line that could be followed by an evil cackle. Sadly, this was no panto. It was the President of the United

---

13 Donald J. Trump on Twitter (7 October 2019).

States of America speaking in real life. And it was delusion.

To be deluded means to have a fixed, false belief that is resistant to the facts or reason. One of the proverbs in the Bible observes:

The rich are wise in their own eyes; one who is poor and discerning sees how deluded they are (Proverbs 28:11).

Donald Trump's style jars, but if you'll forgive me for saying so, there's something of the Donald in us all. Brian Clough used to be a fabulous football manager, but was utterly deluded when he stated on camera, 'When I die, God is going to have to give up His favourite chair.'

You and I may not go as far as to claim that we have great and unmatched wisdom, or to actually say that we are worthy of sitting in God's place. But, functionally, we often operate as if we are God and as if we believe that we possess supreme wisdom.

Like Donald Trump, we are inclined to have an inflated view of our own wisdom and power. We tend to presume that we will usually do the right thing; that we are in charge of our lives;

that we should be able to do whatever we want. And, like Donald, we're a bit deluded.

Our delusion is nothing new. The first ever case was committed by the first man and woman on earth – Adam and Eve. They chose to believe the lie that they could be like God, and so decide for themselves what was good and what was evil.[14]

They knew the facts: God was their Maker; He was in charge. It was absolutely reasonable that, in His world, He should decide what is good and evil. But in a catastrophic moment of delusion, they denied the facts and resisted reason. They believed that they could effectively take charge, deciding for themselves whether something was right or wrong.

Just think about that scenario for a moment – it is *very* appealing. Being in charge. Deciding for yourself what is right and what is wrong. Deciding for yourself what is good and evil. Deciding for yourself what is moral and immoral. Yes, being in charge really appeals! It means that we can move the moral goalposts to wherever *we* like. It means that we can effectively pretend

14 Genesis 3:1–5.

to be God – of our own little universe, in which we are the centre.

But in our delusion we forget who we *really* are. We forget that we are creatures, and instead live and behave as if we are the Creator. We live day-to-day as if we were the ultimate authority, doing what we want and when. Personal mottos include, 'If it feels good, do it,' and, 'No one tells me what to do.'

We are deluded. And yet, in a strange way, we know that. If we look at certain parts of creation – the sky or a mountain or an ocean – we get a very strong sense that we are not God, but are actually very small and weak.

The Bible says:

> ... *what may be known about God is plain ... For since the creation of the world God's invisible qualities – his eternal power and divine nature – have been clearly seen, being understood from what has been made, so that people are without excuse (Romans 1:19–20).*

Those verses tell us that as we observe creation – the things that have 'been made', such as the stars and mountains and flowers and all the animals and human beings – we should know without any doubt that the universe was created by an eternally powerful God. These verses even go so far as to say that creation leaves us *without excuse* for not recognising God's existence.

The complexity, beauty, and precision engineering of creation are like a megaphone loudly proclaiming to each one of us that there is a God, and that our own existence is not the result of merely random phenomena.

So why don't we get that?

Although the testimony of creation is plain for us all to see, the Bible says that we deliberately suppress the truth by our wickedness.[15] We suppress it because we want to run with the delusion that we can be (like) God, and so continue to live as we please – deciding for ourselves what is right and wrong.

The problem here is not ignorance. If that were the case, we'd just need information or education. No, the truth is readily available to us all. We can all see God's glory and power in creation. But we suppress the truth – we bury it.

---

15 Romans 1:18.

We're like a child on the beach who pulls a ring off their sleeping mother's hand, plays with it for a bit, and then buries it in the sand. The ring is still there, but it's now buried and difficult to find.[16] That is, effectively, what we do with the truth about God.

Because we bury the truth about God, we function day-to-day as if we were the highest authority. We play God. And yet the following observation might cause us to take stock.

While we may try our best, we all know that we have not always made right or good or the best decisions. Have you ever chosen to lie or to cheat or to deceive? I have. Have you ever chosen to ignore advice or to arrogantly stand your ground or to be unkind? I have. Have you ever chosen to do a good thing, but done so begrudgingly or for the sake of your own reputation? I have. Not one of us is even close to having always chosen what is right or good or best. I know I'm not. And I know you're not either – even if your name is Donald.

---

16 This illustration was used by Mike Ovey in a Christian doctrine lecture at Oak Hill College, London, 1999.

We like to play God, but it's so obvious that we are not God! If we were God – if we really had great and unmatched wisdom – we would not all have made, and continue to make, such wrong, bad, and weak decisions. Also, as we saw in chapter three, there are millions of things over which we have no control – the weather, traffic, ageing, and other people.

In contrast to us, Jesus only ever does what is right and good and best. As He showed when He came into the world, He always acts with wisdom and integrity. He always tells the truth.

During His time on the earth, He also claimed to be God. Some people thought He was deluded. Others thought He was out of His mind. Some thought He was evil. But Jesus showed that He *was* God by doing amazing and extraordinary and awesome things that only God could do. He spoke as God. When He gave instructions to the weather, what He commanded happened immediately.[17] He acted as God – forgiving sin, healing the sick, and raising the dead. He controlled the things that we cannot control.

---

17 Mark 4:39.

This is how the Bible describes Jesus:

In the past God [the Father] spoke to our forefathers through the prophets at many times and in various ways, but in these last days he has spoken to us by his Son [Jesus], whom he appointed heir of all things, and through whom also he made the universe. The Son is the radiance of God's glory and the exact representation of his being, sustaining all things by his powerful word (Hebrews 1:1–3).

I said earlier that we forget that we are creatures and try to behave as if we are the Creator. But these verses tell us that Jesus is the real Creator – He is the One through whom the universe was made.

To put that another way, Jesus is God! He is God the Son. And that means that He is in full possession of all knowledge. He knows what is right and best and good in any and every situation.

If anyone other than God claims to always have such insight – even with 'great and unmatched wisdom' – then they are foolishly arrogant and painfully deluded. Jesus Christ –

not us, and not Donald Trump – is the One who really does have great and unmatched wisdom. He is God.

And Jesus calls us to stop suppressing the truth and living in the foolish and arrogant delusion that we are God. He calls us to trust Him – the true and living God, who has the right to tell us what is objectively right and wrong, good and evil. He is the One who can really tell us the best way to do life.

Without Jesus, we may think we've got life sorted. We may think that we'll do life right. We may think we're wise. But we're mistaken.

We need the One who is truly great and unmatched in wisdom and power and authority. We need the One who is really God. We need Jesus. Without Him, we have more in common with deluded Donald than we may care to admit.

QUESTIONS TO THINK ABOUT OR DISCUSS

1. Who is in charge of me? Who or what is the source of my wisdom? What

persuades me that they are a good source of wisdom?

2. Do I agree or disagree that all human beings are deluded – that is, inclined to have an inaccurate, inflated view of themselves?

3. What do I make of the Bible's claim that Jesus is God, and that He is the all-knowing source of true wisdom?

4. Am I prepared to investigate whether Jesus is deluded or, as He claimed, divine?

7

THE FAITH
IN US ALL

Lots of people say that they don't have any faith. Some wish they did, but as far as they can tell, it's just not part of who they are. Faith seems to have bypassed them. Others are very clear that they don't want any faith.

In actual fact, we don't really have any choice. Faith is something we all have, whether we like it or not. It is common to all human beings. Sure, we don't have a common faith, but we do all have faith and we exercise our faith in lots of ways every single day.

To have faith is to believe in or to put your trust in something or someone. Every time we sit down, we put our faith in the chair to hold us up – I'm presuming you don't go through a thorough safety inspection with every chair that you are about to sit on for the first time. We sit on it by faith. If, however, the chair was made out of limp lettuce leaves that look like they've just fallen out of a Big Mac, I imagine we would think twice about putting our faith in (and weight on) it.

At other times we exercise our faith in more serious situations. Whenever we get on a bus, we put our faith in the driver to transport us safely. Before getting on board, I have never asked a bus driver if he would mind showing me his driving licence. I have believed and trusted that the driver was proficient in driving busses.

And what about flying? To put it mildly, it would be extremely dangerous to travel on an aeroplane if the person up front did not know what they were doing. But again, not once have I asked to see proof that the pilot was suitably qualified. By getting on board, I have put my faith in both the pilot's ability and in the airline's training and assessment of her. I have believed and trusted that she knew what she was doing – all with zero evidence.

Every single day we all put faith in people we have never met, and in things that we have never seen. The issue, then, is not whether or not we have faith, but who or what we put our faith in. Who or what do we believe in? Who or what will we trust?

That poses another question: who or what is really trustworthy? Or to put that another way, who or what is worthy of my faith?

Money seems like an attractive contender. It certainly opens up opportunities for those who have it. But it is also very limited. It could buy you excellent healthcare – but it can't always buy you good health. It could make you popular – but it can't give you true friendship. It could buy you good things – but it can't make you good. While money is really useful, it won't deliver ultimate things. It can't give us life, and it is useless in death.

What else might we put our faith in? 'Believe in yourself' has become a modern mantra in our Western post-God culture. Those three words were written twice – presumably for emphasis –

on the wall of one school hall for every student to see during their daily assembly. I'm all for encouraging children to have a positive view of themselves – each one is a precious human being. But believing in self can be foolish. Faith in self puts 'me' at the centre of my universe and encourages unhelpful – possibly delusional – self-sufficiency. You see, regardless of how much we believe in ourselves, we will realise at some point that we can't achieve all that we would like to – or, indeed, all that others would like us to accomplish. And so, if we keep on believing in ourselves, we will either end up being deluded about what we can *really* do, or depressed when we don't succeed.

Repeated failure may, in the end, only lead to us believing that we are a let-down. Ironically, that would result in having a low view of self – the very opposite of what was intended by the slogan.

I don't mind acknowledging that I know that I can't fully trust myself. There are very many occasions when I would have loved to have reacted graciously, generously, kindly, selflessly, respectfully, gently, honestly, or with self-control. But I didn't.

Despite the mantra to believe in ourselves, we can't fully trust ourselves to always do what's right. Often we don't – which is partly why, in one way or another, our lives are messy, and we carry with us lots of painful and regretful baggage.

Given that human beings are essentially the same, then it follows that we can't fully trust anyone else either. The Bible warns us:

Do not put your trust in princes,
    in human beings, who cannot save.
(Psalm 146:3)

Don't trust princes. For that matter, don't trust presidents or prime ministers either! Don't trust sports stars or celebrities or other high flyers. In particular, don't trust people to do what only God can do: to save.

The Bible is telling us that it's a mistake to put our trust – our faith – in human beings because they cannot save us. They cannot give us the life we all desire. They cannot always be there for us. They do not rule over all the circumstances of life. They are largely powerless to always do for us what we want, or to always be what we want them to be.

How strange, then, that we tend to trust people to do for us what only God can do! What a burden of expectation we put on one another – usually on our spouse or parents or children or best friend. We want them to make us feel happy; we want them to make us feel fulfilled; we want them to give us purpose; we want them to make things better for us when we hurt. Sometimes they may be able to do these things – to some degree – but not always, and not forever.

Of course, personal relationships are a huge blessing and joy. It's not good for us to be alone. It's great to do life with others in close, meaningful relationship based on mutual love, respect, and trust. We are to help, support, and encourage one another. We are to be faithful to one another and trustworthy.

But other human beings are not worthy of ultimate faith because, just like us, they cannot always be there; they are not always good; they are not all-powerful; and they are not always faithful.

That same psalm continues by saying:

Blessed are those whose help is the God of Jacob,
*   whose hope is in the LORD their God.*

He is the Maker of heaven and earth,
the sea, and everything in them –
he remains faithful for ever.
(Psalm 146:5–6)

Here is someone who is worthy of our faith, someone who remains faithful forever: God, the Maker of heaven and earth. And there is great blessing in putting our faith in the God who is forever faithful. Elsewhere we are told:

But blessed is the one who trusts in the Lord,
whose confidence is in him.
They will be like a tree planted by the water
that sends out its roots by the stream.
It does not fear when heat comes;
its leaves are always green.
It has no worries in a year of drought
and never fails to bear fruit.
(Jeremiah 17:7–8)

Trusting God is to be like a tree planted by a stream. It is truly nourishing, fruitful, and life-giving.

As the Bible proceeds, it reveals that, together with God the Father, Jesus – God the Son – should be the supreme object of our trust or faith. The Lord Jesus Christ is truly trustworthy and utterly faithful. And the life He gives to those who put their faith in Him is eternal. The most famous verse in the Bible says:

> *For God so loved the world that he gave his one and only Son, that whoever believes in him shall not perish but have eternal life (John 3:16).*

We can't trust money or things or other people to give us life. They may slightly extend our short lives, but they can't give us eternal life. They can't deal with death. But Jesus can. Therefore the Bible urges us to believe in Him – to make Him the object of our faith so that we may be right with God and eternally safe.

As people saw what Jesus did and heard what He taught, they put their faith in Him. They believed that He was God. They believed that He was the Saviour that they needed. They believed He had beaten death and was able to give new life – eternal life – to all who put their faith in Him. And for the very same reasons, people ever since have been putting their faith in Him too.

There's no doubt about it: we all have faith. What we have to decide now is: in what or whom we will put our faith?

QUESTIONS TO THINK ABOUT OR DISCUSS

1. Which people, or what things, do I put my faith in?

2. What do they give me? Are they consistent – always available and always able? What can't they do for me?

3. What's the problem with making myself the object of my faith?

4. What do I think about the Bible's encouragement to put my faith or belief in Jesus?

8

THE WORSHIPPER
IN US ALL

It was a beautiful moment in our kitchen: 'Dad, are you a better cook than Mum?' It was made even more wonderful by the fact that my wife, Sharon, was there too. Every day she provides our family with tasty, nutritious, and nicely presented food. So why the serious question? I had just cooked our kids their first ever 'Jacko special' – one of my two 'recipes'. Without wanting to give too much away, it involves toast, baked beans, grated cheese, and a poached egg! Instantly, the kids knew this was a *very* special meal! They loved it. We all love it.

I wouldn't call myself a cook, but I still cooked that meal. I wouldn't call myself a swimmer, but I can swim. You may not call yourself a worshipper, but you still worship.

You may not regard yourself as 'the religious type'. Not many do. I accept that. But we are still worshippers because, however irreligious we consider ourselves to be, we still worship. Every day. All of us.

It's part of who we are. So the truth is that we just can't help worshipping – anymore than we can help breathing.

The word 'worship' stems from the word 'worth'. We worship the person or thing to whom or which we attribute most worth or value.

Who or what do you value most?

You may immediately know the answer. If not, think about how much you invest your thoughts, time, energy, money, and emotion in someone or something. What do you daydream about? Who or what has the greatest influence on how you choose to live? Who or what is your life organised around? Perhaps it's your work or your hobby or your family or training or gaming or drinking or good nights out?

To put it another way, what would you be most afraid to lose? Answering that question might help to reveal the particular object(s) of *your* worship.

It's often easier to see what other people, rather than ourselves, worship. Some worship their home or garden; that's what carries most worth to them. Spare thoughts are given to pondering the next improvement, the next design, the next feature. And spare income will be spent on it too.

Many worship their sport – whether it's one they play or watch. Going to a football match is quite like going to church in that the congregation (fans) gather for a communal act of worship. Arms aloft, they sing heartfelt songs of praise to their team. They make sacrificial acts of devotion, spending thousands of pounds on season tickets, replica kits, and travelling all around the country (and even the world) to watch them.

Lots of us effectively worship our children. Our lives can revolve around them – *their* happiness, *their* sporting or social activities, *their* advancement. We might make huge sacrifices for them – perhaps even going into debt to give them what they want, or what we think will make them happy or successful. We might make our relationship to our children our supreme relationship.

Home, garden, sport, children – these are just a few obvious contenders, but the object of our worship could be pretty much anything. Perhaps our car, bike, pets, career, hobby, qualifications, reputation, computer games, food, holidays, pleasure, or beauty. You name it, people will have idolised and worshipped it.

And then there is arguably our favourite object of worship: ourselves. Self-worship is seen in devotion to our own personal comfort, ease, happiness, fulfilment, satisfaction, and control.

So we are all worshippers, not least because we were all made to worship God. Even if we don't actually worship Him, it doesn't mean that we don't worship. It just means that we worship something or someone else.

Before going any further, we should note that most of what we worship are really, really good things or relationships given to us by God to enjoy. We should not feel the least bit guilty about enjoying them!

The issue comes when those good things overreach themselves and become 'god-things'. When we allow them to take that place in our heart and life that rightly belongs to God. When they become ruling things. When they effectively become substitute gods – the things or people that we look to for identity, fulfilment, meaning, purpose, hope, happiness, security, status, or significance.

The Bible says about all humanity:

For although they knew God, they neither glorified him as God nor gave thanks to him, but their thinking became futile and their foolish hearts were darkened (Romans 1:21).

These words tell us that when we don't treat God as God, our thinking becomes futile. This leads to us worshipping things that are not worthy of worship – because they themselves are futile:

They exchanged the truth of God for a lie, and worshipped and served created things rather than the Creator (Romans 1:25).

While the world is full of worship and full of worshippers, our worship is often misplaced. We have been hijacked. We typically use that term when an illegitimate person or group takes control of an aeroplane and redirects it to where they want to go. That's what has happened in our hearts. They have been hijacked by all kinds of things that have taken control and point us in a bad direction – such that we are more inclined to worship created things rather than our Creator.

As I said before, many created things are great gifts from God that can give us huge pleasure. He has made them to be a blessing to us. But they must be enjoyed in their right place – somewhere beneath our Creator. The *worship* of created things – letting them be first in our hearts – is ultimately futile because God didn't design them to give us supreme satisfaction. They are powerless to help us in ultimate ways. They can't give life. They can't give us unending joy. And they are little or no help in death.

The Bible spells out the futility of centring our lives on things that have been made:

The idols of the nations are silver and gold
  made by human hands.
They have mouths, but cannot speak,
  eyes, but cannot see.
They have ears, but cannot hear,
  nor is there breath in their mouths.
Those who make them will be like them
  and so will all who trust in them.
(Psalm 135:15–18)

What a sobering thought! If we worship created things – things without breath; in other words, dead things – then one day we will be like them. We will be dead. We will be as powerless and useless as our idol. Even the living people we may idolise are extremely limited in what they can do – limited by their knowledge, strength, influence, money, time, and energy – and one day they too will die.

But Jesus was not, and is not, limited. He clearly showed Himself to be the Lord of all creation. When He spoke, the wind and waves instantly obeyed Him. And though He died, He also rose from the grave – showing His authority even over death. He repeatedly demonstrated the words proclaimed at His birth – that He is 'God with us'.[18]

Here, then, is someone who is truly worthy of worship – because He is the Lord of everything and everyone. The Bible not only records numerous occasions when people did worship Jesus,[19] but that even angels worship Him.[20]

When those people worshipped Jesus, He didn't stop them or accuse them of idolatry. He accepted their worship – because as the divine Son of God, He was worthy of worship. And He is worthy of worship today. Our worship. What's more, the Bible says that, one day, everyone *will* worship Him:

> … *at the name of Jesus every knee should bow,*
>   *in heaven and on earth and under*
>   *the earth,*
> *and every tongue acknowledge that Jesus*
> *Christ is Lord,*
>   *to the glory of God the Father.*
> *(Philippians 2:10–11)*

---

18 Matthew 1:23.
19 Matthew 14:33; 28:9, 17; John 9:38.
20 Hebrews 1:6.

This is where we are all heading: a day of worship! A day when we shall all worship Jesus – every knee shall bow before Him, and every tongue will acknowledge that He is Lord. It will be the greatest act of worship in the history of the world. And every single one of us will be part of it.

For some it will be the most glorious occasion – a day of vindication as all humanity acknowledges that Jesus really is Lord and God. For others it will be a devastating day – as they realise that their worship in life was utterly misplaced and futile. They had worshipped created things instead of their Creator – and now they will face His right and fair judgement upon them.

But it doesn't have to be like that. Jesus is not just the Lord who deserves our worship. He came into the world to be the loving Saviour of all who will believe and trust in Him. When we do that – when we believe and trust in Jesus as our personal Lord and Saviour – it leads to the right kind of worship.

Here's the big truth to take on board from all this: it is better to worship Jesus sooner rather than later. It is better to see who Jesus is now and to worship Him as He deserves before being forced to worship Him on the last day. Don't be too easily pleased with creation and ignore the Creator. Don't be too easily pleased with your savings (or whatever you have bought with them) and ignore the Saviour.

We are all worshippers – even if we wouldn't normally use that word. The question is who or what will be the object of *our* worship?

QUESTIONS TO THINK ABOUT OR DISCUSS

1. Who or what do I love most? What takes up most of my thoughts or resources? What do I daydream about? What things are currently the objects of my worship?

2. What is my response to the biblical claim that our worship of created things is misplaced and that, actually, Jesus should be the object of our worship?

3. What do I think about the prospect that we all will worship Jesus?

4. Am I ready to investigate the biblical claims for Jesus and to think about whether I should worship Him sooner rather than later?

9

THE DEPENDENCY IN US ALL

My wife had been taken to get cleaned and stitched up. Enough said. I was left alone with our new son in the room where he had just been born. I'd only been a dad for about half an hour. The responsibility weighed on me: here was a precious little person who couldn't do anything for himself except breathe. Apart from that, he was completely dependent on others. Unfortunately for him, I was the only other person in the room – and already I was struggling! Thankfully, the door opened and in came a lady pushing a trolley with mugs and a pot of tea.

'Do you happen to know how this thing works?' I asked, holding aloft the nappy that the midwife had handed me before wheeling Sharon down the corridor. The tea lady kindly showed me which way round the nappy went and how it fastened. What a genius bit of kit!

Fast-forward a few years and I could only watch from a distance as my dear old mum became increasingly dependent. No longer able to cook her own meals, she depended on someone delivering frozen meals that could be heated in the microwave. No longer able to clean her house, she depended on a cleaner who came each week. No longer able to climb the stairs, she depended on a stairlift to get her up to her bedroom. Eventually, she wasn't able to even get into bed by herself – she depended on carers to help. There was so much, at the end of her life, which she was simply unable to do. And so each day she depended on a few outstandingly good friends, her family, and some fabulous healthcare professionals for the help that she needed.

My son was born utterly dependent on others. My mum died utterly dependent on others.

And despite being relatively healthy, fit, and capable, I was dependent on others too – not least the tea lady!

When you think about it, we are so dependent on others not just at the start and end of life, but every day. We depend on teachers to teach us; on doctors to rightly diagnose our symptoms and to prescribe the correct treatment; on water companies to keep us hydrated and clean; on energy companies to send us power with which to heat our homes and cook our food; on farmers and supply chains and supermarkets to keep our cupboards full and our bellies satisfied; on communication companies to keep us online and in touch; on bus and train drivers to get us where we want to go; on all the people who collect our rubbish, repair the roads, produce the products we want to buy, or who care enough about us to watch our back.

We even refer to those closest to us as our 'dependants'. They depend or rely on us in some way.

We start life dependent. We end life dependent. What do you reckon we're supposed to be between those two points? The answer is obvious: we are to be dependent. Our lives begin, continue, and eventually end in a state of dependency.

How strange, then, that we so desperately try to live independently. We imagine that we can do life by ourselves; that we don't need anyone else. Picture teenagers striving for independence. But they don't really want to be independent – not truly independent. They just want to be less dependent on their parents than they were. Independence is a complete fallacy.

My kids and I love watching Ed Stafford programmes together. He is a survivalist. Think Bear Grylls on steroids. Ed's only kit comprises a few cameras to film his experience, a small medical kit, and a satellite phone in case of emergency. When I say 'only kit', I literally mean 'only kit'. You see, Ed Stafford often goes into jungles or deserts or mountains stark naked. No shoes. No clothes. No water. No food. No knife. And he survives. His aim is more than that: to thrive, which sometimes he does – sort of! Usually his expeditions last about a week or so, but the longest was sixty days on a desert island. What a guy!

Even then, of course, he is still dependent – on his environment. He's dependent on there being a suitable source of water; on an animal walking or swimming into one of his traps so that he can eat; on there being suitable material for making a shelter; on there being enough wood to make a fire – and on the sun to dry enough tinder and kindling to get it going.

One thing that each of his expeditions has in common (besides the lack of kit) is that, by the end, he is clearly ready for home and to see his family again.

Sooner or later even the best survivors need the help of others. Independence is exhausting and lonely. And there's a reason for that: human beings were not designed to be independent. We were designed to be dependent on God, and interdependent on one another. Being dependent is thoroughly human. It's normal. It's good. It is not something to be ashamed of, despise, or resist.

In contrast to us, God is not dependent. The Bible says:

The God who made the world and everything in it is the Lord of heaven and earth and does not live in temples built by human hands. And he is not served by human hands, as if he needed anything. Rather, he himself gives everyone life and breath and everything else (Acts 17:24–25).

That's quite sobering. We like to imagine that we are self-sufficient, but we're not. The Bible asserts that God made us and that He has given us 'life and breath and everything else'.

Every breath we take is a gift from God. Without His say so, we would not so much as have a whiff of air in our lungs. We would not have life. And everything else we have or do is only because God has given it to us or enabled us. There is really no such thing as a 'self-made man' – or a self-made woman for that matter.

Whenever he was helped, my youngest son would often say, 'I can do it' – meaning, 'Leave me alone; I don't want your help.' But the truth was different. He couldn't do his coat zip up; he couldn't tie the cord that would hold his trousers up; and he couldn't always put his shoes on the right feet. He needed help.

We all do something similar with God. We effectively say, 'I can do it; leave me alone; I don't want you.'

But even the most independent, self-sufficient person will need help at some point. Sooner or later our physical, practical, financial, or emotional limitations will be exposed.

Jesus told a famous story – commonly known as 'The parable of the prodigal (or lost) son'.[21] It concerns a young man who thought that his life would be better if he were independent of his father, so he asked his dad to give him his inheritance early. So much for independence! He was reliant on his dad's money. But he then promptly squandered it on fast food, fast cars, fast horses, and fast women. When the cash dried up, his friends dried up too, and he quickly hit rock bottom. He took a job feeding pigs, and was so poor that even the pigs' food looked appetising. It was time for some fast thinking.

The truly wonderful moment in the story is when the young man came to his senses. He realised that his father's hired servants had food to spare, while he was starving to death. And so he went back to his father – planning to offer himself as a servant instead of being a son.

---

21 Luke 15:11–31.

But his father was looking out for him. He knew that his son could not survive independently. He knew that he would make a foolish mess of life. And when he saw his son in the distance, we're told that he was filled with compassion. He ran to his son, threw his arms around him, and kissed him.

It's a parable about God and us. Like that son, we need, rely on, take, and enjoy God's good things. But we want them without God. We think we can do better independently. We can't.

It illustrates the very humbling message of the whole Bible: that we cannot make it on our own. We were made for God. We need God. Whether we like it or not, we are dependent on God – He gives us life and breath and everything else. And so trying to live independently from Him is foolish. In the end it leads to ruin and disaster. Self-reliance is a fallacy that leads us to the very worst independence: separation from God for all eternity – which the Bible calls 'hell'.

But that is not what God wants. He loves us so much. His heart is full of compassion for us. And through His Son Jesus Christ, He came looking for us.

Have you realised yet that independence is impossible? That ultimately we are all dependent? We are dependent on God not only for everything, but also for salvation from the folly of seeking to live independently from Him.

Perhaps you're still far away from God – trying to live independently. You enjoy His gifts and resources, but never really give Him a second thought. Or maybe you've hit rock bottom and are not sure which way to turn. Perhaps you've reached the point where you realise that life without God – which promised so much – hasn't really delivered. Maybe you're looking for the road home.

The good news of the Christian faith is that, through Jesus, we can come back home to God. We can have a right relationship with the One who made us and who loves us so deeply. God longs for us to come to our senses and to come home to Him, our heavenly Father. He is the God who made the world and everything in it, and on whom we depend for life and breath and everything else!

QUESTIONS TO THINK ABOUT OR DISCUSS

1. On whom or what do I depend?

2. How do I express independence from God?

3. What do I think of the idea that I am dependent on God for life, breath, and everything else?

4. Do I want to come home to God?

10

THE FEAR IN US ALL

Apparently, twelve years is quite a long time to avoid the dentist. My teeth seemed fine. Why waste the dentist's time? Or mine? But the real issue was not being reluctant to waste time. It was dentophobia. I was frightened. I would have happily avoided the dentist for twenty-five years. To my mind, twelve was not nearly long enough!

A good friend knew about this little foible, so when he booked a dental check-up for himself, he asked if I would like to go too. In a moment of almost extraordinary bravery, I agreed.

Fear is never as intense when someone else is with you.

Wouldn't it be great if someone could be with us whenever we are afraid? Reassuring us. Dispelling our fear. Because we are all afraid – of something. However hard or tough or measured we think we are, things will frighten us.

Some fears are rational and understandable. Others are irrational, but no less real. People can be afraid of spiders, large crowds, small spaces, the dark – and the dentist! Some fear not having what they want, or not having enough, or being alone. So-called FOMOs are constantly checking their phone for Fear Of Missing Out. Others don't fear missing out, but being found out – they are haunted by the past. Still others are frightened by the future.

Every single one of us will know that feeling of fear. Perhaps someone once jumped out on you as a prank. Perhaps you have been threatened – either physically or with legal action, or have unwittingly got yourself into a dangerous situation. Maybe you have received an unfavourable medical diagnosis. These are all frightening.

And what about our fear of other people? Not just terrorists and criminals, but 'ordinary' people – even our friends and neighbours.

We fear what they think of us. We want to be liked. We fear making a social blunder that will cause people to think ill of us. We fear for our reputation. We fear not being loved.

This has been magnified through social media. Ironically, we may have hundreds of virtual 'friends', but there is a certain degree of fear attached. You can understand why. Countless people have apparently posted the wrong thing or shared a picture of themselves doing something that, in the court of social media opinion, is deemed inappropriate. Within a matter of hours they end up being utterly shamed and humiliated as their 'crime' is shared around the world. Just the thought of that happening to us is frightening.

As well as being a fabulous place, the world is also a fearful place – spoiled by war, terrorism, crime, unfaithfulness, loss, and disease. Sometimes fear can rule over us and paralyse us. Very often the things we fear effectively control us. But they are terrible masters: when you fear missing out, you can't put your phone down. When you fear other people, you desperately try to please them – even if they disrespect you or treat you badly. When you fear not having enough, you work every hour God sends. When you fear the dentist, you avoid going – even though it may result in more damage to your teeth.

Of course, fear is not always negative. Sometimes it's protective. The fear of having a horrible road accident causes us to make sure we have decent lights on our bike when out at night, or that our car is in good repair. Adrenalin junkies who enjoy extreme sports testify to how fear helps to keep them safe. It heightens their awareness of danger and enables them to focus, concentrate, and so, hopefully, avoid imminent death. Fear protects us all to some degree. It prompts caution.

The Bible talks of this good kind of fear – a fear to be safe and avoid death:

The fear of the LORD is a fountain of life,
*   turning a person from the snares of death.*
(Proverbs 14:27)

Fearing God protects us from death. It's 'a fountain of life'.

'The fear of the LORD' is not about being terrified of God. It's relating to Him in the right way – recognising that He is very big and powerful and awesome, while we are very small, weak, and, frankly, a bit ludicrous! God is not a long-bearded, impotent, old man. He should not be ignored or treated with contempt. He should be feared and revered.

In many ways fearing God in this way – recognising who He is and what He is like – is very similar indeed to what other parts of the Bible call 'faith'. It is trusting God because He is big and powerful and good and all-knowing – so He is the One to run to and to trust! Fearing the Lord does not suddenly remove all our other fears, but it does help us to face them – because we do so with the One who is supremely powerful and who rules over all.

And, incredibly, fearing and trusting in the Lord also saves us from our greatest fear: 'the snares of death'. As I have already said, we don't like to talk about this issue. We avoid using the 'D word' – preferring to say that someone has 'passed away'. But we are increasingly aware that, however we want to describe death, we are all heading towards it. Generally we see death as a very unpleasant and unappealing prospect. Most of us would gladly leave the queue – if that were possible. Even if we imagine just 'quietly slipping away in our sleep', we still dread death because it will take everything we love from us. For many death is terrifying.

That is why it is so wonderful that the Bible tackles this fear head on. The first few chapters of the Bible record the first human fear – brought about by humanity not trusting God and so choosing to disobey Him.[22] It eventually led to death. And the Bible ends with the supremely terrifying prospect of all those who reject God being eternally separated from God – referred to as 'the second death'.[23] But gloriously, between those two points, the rest of the Bible repeatedly reveals how we human beings can come back to God as our loving heavenly Father. It shows how we can approach Him with confidence; how we can have confidence in the face of death; how we can have eternal life; and how we can be set free from fear.

It is all possible and available through Jesus:

---

22 Genesis 3:1–10.
23 Revelation 20:14–15.

*Since the children have flesh and blood, he
[Jesus] too shared in their humanity so that
by his death he might break the power of
him who holds the power of death – that is,
the devil – and free those who all their lives
were held in slavery by their fear of death
(Hebrews 2:14–15).*

Jesus died for people who are afraid and enslaved
– people who are held in slavery by their fear of
death. His death sets us free from our own fear
of death.

Many of us fear death because we are aware
that we have not lived a good life, and so we fear
the prospect of meeting God and being judged
by Him. But Jesus died to pay the full penalty for
our sin so that we don't have to do so. He died for
those who are afraid of their past and afraid of
being found out. His death ultimately deals with
all our guilt and shame. That's why believing in
Jesus is so important and so liberating.

The devil likes to accuse people of their guilt[24]
– which, given the bad things that we think, say,
and do, is very easy for him. His accusations are

---

24 Zechariah 3:1; Revelation 12:10.

often right. In that sense, he has power over us and a hold on us. But his power and hold were broken when Jesus died. So, the devil can accuse all he likes, but all who come to believe and trust in Jesus should have no fear of being judged. At the cross, the day of judgement for their sin has already taken place. And being just, God will not judge their sin again. They are free! God welcomes them as His dearly loved children who need no longer fear meeting Him.

Wonderfully, this also sets us free from the fear of other people. If God has accepted us, then who cares if mere human beings – with all their flaws and weaknesses (that are almost certainly very similar to our own) – do not?

But there is more. When Jesus rose from the dead, death itself was defeated. For those who believe in Him, death is not the end. Jesus Himself said:

> *I am the resurrection and the life. The one who believes in me will live, even though they die* (John 11:25).

His resurrection quells our fears by showing that death is merely a stepping stone to glorious and eternal life with Him. The risen Lord Jesus encouraged His followers with these words:

> *Do not be afraid. I am the First and the Last. I am the Living One; I was dead, and now look, I am alive for ever and ever! And I hold the keys of death and Hades [the place of death] (Revelation 1:17–18).*

'Do not be afraid' is the most common command in the Bible – appearing well over a hundred times! God knew that we would be afraid in life, but He doesn't want us to remain afraid – not even of death.

A wise man once told me to only have one key for my shed. It means that I'm in charge of it. No one else can put anything in or take anything out without my say so.

Jesus holds the keys to death and Hades. And He is the only keyholder, for only He has beaten death. No one can escape without Him. But for those who trust Jesus, death is suddenly not the fearful prospect it once was. Jesus has the keys to set us free and give us life! And He has promised that He will.

One person helpfully put it like this: 'Consider what an advantage it is that Jesus Christ has been raised from the dead. When you pray to Him, he can answer. When you are sick, he can heal you. When you are in trouble, he can save you. When you sin, he can forgive you. And when you are dead, he can bring you back to life.'[25]

When we believe and trust in this risen and reigning Lord Jesus, we do not need to be afraid. Fear is never as intense when someone else is with you – and especially when that someone is Jesus!

QUESTIONS TO THINK ABOUT OR DISCUSS

1. What or whom do I fear?

2. Does that fear control me in any way?

3. How do I deal with my fears?

4. What do I think about Jesus' offer to set me free from fear – including from the fear of death?

---

25 Philip Graham Ryken, *Jeremiah and Lamentations: From Sorrow to Hope* (Crossway, 2001), p. 190.

11

THE SHAME
IN US ALL

Scandal is never far from the news. Celebrities, sports stars, politicians, and religious leaders are easy targets. Often held up as role models, no time is wasted when they mess up. Photos or video clips quickly circulate on social media – apparently providing evidence of an illicit affair, abuse, cheating, drug taking, or something similar – and are then picked up by the press and television channels. The individuals concerned are very publicly shamed.

The 2009 parliamentary expenses scandal saw twenty-two Members of Parliament resign.

Eight MPs and peers faced criminal charges for false accounting and fraud. Seven went to prison.[26] They had used taxpayers' money to pay for swimming pool maintenance, second home refurbishment, and even a floating duck house for a garden lake! It was undoubtedly a shameful time for British politics.

What do you imagine was going on in their hearts when they fraudulently claimed excessive or inappropriate expenses? We can't know for certain, but we tend to want as much as possible of whatever we perceive to be good – and sometimes we will behave badly to get it. Often it comes down to plain and simple greed. Greed is a shameful thing. But it is not just an issue for politicians.

We could cite so-called 'fat cat' CEOs who pay themselves vast, often disproportionate, multi-million-pound bonuses. Or the bankers and stock-market traders who arrogantly and recklessly gamble – resulting in a major economic recession in 2008. Or middle-class, self-employed workers who fiddle their tax return. Or working-

26 https://en.wikipedia.org/wiki/United_Kingdom_
   parliamentary_expenses_scandal#Criminal_charges
   (accessed on 7 February 2022).

class tradesmen who do 'cash-in-hand' jobs so as to avoid paying tax. Or people who fraudulently claim disability benefits while being fit enough to play sport.

In all the situations described above, the amounts of money involved may be quite different, but the heart issue is the same.

Every section of society is affected by greed, but that greed also happens at a personal level. We see it at play when we have plenty, but still desire more or bigger. We want more than we need: more cake, more clothes, a bigger house, a bigger car, more gadgets, more toys, a bigger portion, a bigger garden, more money, more stuff.

I imagine that it was partly that desire for more or bigger that caused our MPs – our national representatives – to behave so badly. But as they did so, they represented us very well indeed! And there are other areas in which we are not so different from those who are publicly shamed.

When a public figure is found to have lied in court or to a public inquiry, it's shameful – but they are not alone in lying. Although very few people would actually call themselves a liar, I don't know anyone who would say that they have not told lies. Perhaps you feel ashamed of your lies – or you would do if they were more widely known? There may be differences in the degree to which we are guilty, but the heart issue – in this case, deceitfulness – is identical.

And what about shameful cheating, pride, anger, immorality, rudeness, envy, hypocrisy, double standards, and the like? It shouldn't take us too much thought to be able to *personally* tick those boxes too.

The point is this: when it comes to shame, we have more in common with those who have been exposed than not. The difference might just be we have a lower profile or have not been caught.

Human shame is not a new issue. The early chapters of the Bible tell us that when the first man and woman disobeyed God, they suddenly became aware of their nakedness and felt ashamed.[27] God responded so graciously by covering their shame – by kindly clothing them![28]

Since then, all people have felt shame – and for good reason.

---

27 Genesis 2:25; 3:10.
28 Genesis 3:21.

Jesus knows that we all have a lot to be ashamed of – even if this is not how we see ourselves. Addressing some religious people who proudly thought that they were better than others, He said:

> *What comes out of a person is what defiles them. For it is from within, out of a person's heart, that evil thoughts come – sexual immorality, theft, murder, adultery, greed, malice, deceit, lewdness, envy, slander, arrogance and folly (Mark 7:20–22).*

These are shocking words! They were spoken to people who, on the surface, *appeared* to be really good. But Jesus taught them that, on the inside, every human heart is a factory of evil.

That verdict may sound harsh, but it is certainly true that lots of horrible things come out of us. And, says Jesus, that happens for the simple reason that they are already in us.

This grates with me – and perhaps it grates with you too – but I don't have to reflect on Jesus' words for very long to know that this is what my heart is really like. It's a cesspit. There are so many things that I said or did as a child, and as a teenager, and as a young man for which I feel rightly ashamed. This is still the case now as a husband, and as a dad, and as a church pastor. These things make me cringe. Some are hauntingly etched in my memory. And my catalogue of shame continues to grow.

No doubt, there are things for which you too have a sense of shame. Maybe things that no one else knows about – times when you have been unkind, greedy, immoral, angry, arrogant, selfish, or deceitful. Perhaps those things haunt you. As much as you try, you just can't forget them.

Top sports stars and celebrities have their names in a virtual 'hall of fame'. If we're honest, all of us could rightly have our names in a 'hall of shame'.

Shame is wretched. We feel ashamed of ourselves. But we also feel an intense, ongoing embarrassment before others. Our shame is personal and, in its worst form, social. It often has a public dimension to do with what others think of us, making us feel like we don't (or can't) belong. We feel ostracised; unacceptable; humiliated; unwanted – or would do if our darkest deeds were made known.

That's why some people seek court injunctions to prevent certain details of their lives being revealed. They are attempting to avoid public shame.

But listen to Jesus' beautiful words to those who are rightly ashamed. On one occasion, a woman was brought to Jesus who had been caught in adultery. Her shame was very great and very public. She would have been a social outcast. And according to the law back then, her guilt required that she be stoned to death. Jesus said to her religious accusers: 'Let any one of you who is without sin be the first to throw a stone at her.'[29]

No one did. So Jesus asked the woman:

'Has no one condemned you?'
'No one, sir,' she said.
'Then neither do I condemn you … Go now and leave your life of sin' (John 8:10–11).

Then, in the very next verse, Jesus continues:

---

29 John 8:7.

I am the light of the world. Whoever follows
me will never walk in darkness, but will have
the light of life (John 8:12).

Light exposes things. But when you know you
have done (or are doing) wrong things, you don't
really want the light to be turned on. John, one
of Jesus' disciples, wrote:

... light has come into the world, but people
loved darkness instead of light because their
deeds were evil. Everyone who does evil hates
the light, and will not come into the light
for fear that their deeds will be exposed. But
whoever lives by the truth comes into the light
(John 3:19–21).

Darkness gives people cover – which is why
many thieves operate at night. But remaining
in darkness means living with guilt and the fear
of shame – hoping that we'll not be found out
and exposed.

Being exposed by the press would be painful.
The press don't love those they expose. Quite the
opposite: they love salacious stories, increased
sales, and maximum humiliation of their target.

But being exposed by Jesus, the Light of the world, is different. It may also be painful, but despite what we've done, Jesus loves us. He loves us more than anyone has ever loved us. And He offers us forgiveness instead of condemnation, restoration instead of humiliation, and, crucially, the opportunity for our story to change.

We saw earlier that the first man and woman felt ashamed because of their sin and nakedness, but that God lovingly covered their shame. He clothed them with garments of skin, which would have involved the death of an animal. Their shame was covered through sacrifice. It was a little pointer to how He would lovingly and graciously cover our shame through the willing sacrifice of His Son, Jesus.

As the completely innocent Lord Jesus hung publicly and naked on a Roman cross, He bore our sin and shame – all of it – in our place. It is by His sacrifice that our shame may be covered. The Bible even talks about those who believe in Jesus as being clothed with Christ.[30] This may sound strange, but just means that when God looks at me with all my shame, He instead sees

---

30 Galatians 3:27.

the innocent life of Christ. Basically, on the cross Jesus was treated as if He were me – guilty and full of shame – so that I may be treated by God the Father as if I were Christ – completely innocent.

The Bible says:

For the joy that was set before him [Jesus] he endured the cross, scorning its shame (Hebrews 12:2).

Jesus endured the cross. He faced the shame and humiliation that sin deserves, so that we who are guilty – we who have done shameful things – do not, ultimately, have to do so.

And Jesus now urges us to come to Him, the Light, to receive the forgiveness and the righteousness that He has won for us. Our shame is not a problem for Him; He is able to deal with it. And as we bring it to Him, He embraces us.

It means being honest about what we are like. Admitting our guilt. Acknowledging our shame. Shame makes us feel like we can't belong, but Jesus welcomes us, loves us, and accepts us. Guilt makes us feel condemned, but when we come to Jesus in faith, He does not condemn us; He forgives us! And then He patiently helps us to do what He told that woman to do: to change; to leave our life of sin.

So here's our choice: we can continue to secretly harbour our shame. We can remain in darkness – perhaps even keeping up an appearance of respectability, hoping that we can keep the lid on whatever lurks beneath the surface. We might be able to do that pretty well. But we won't get away with it forever, because a day is coming when we will all stand before God and everything will be exposed.

Alternatively, we can come into the light, admit what we're like, and receive what is on offer – knowing that whatever is exposed, Jesus' death on the cross covers it!

If we say that we have no sin, we deceive ourselves, and the truth is not in us. If we confess our sins, he is faithful and just and will forgive us our sins and purify us from all unrighteousness (1 John 1:8–9).

The fact that Jesus willingly faced the shame that our sin deserves is often described as the 'scandal of the cross'. It is utterly scandalous! Wonderfully scandalous!

QUESTIONS TO THINK ABOUT OR DISCUSS

1. What am I ashamed of? What would I rather was never exposed?

2. What – if anything – do I think is the consequence of my shame and guilt?

3. How do I think or hope my guilt might be dealt with?

4. What do I think of Jesus' offer to deal with my guilt for me?

12

THE LAWYER
IN US ALL

What do you do when someone has accused you unfairly or treated you badly? I'll tell you what I do: in my mind, I prosecute them. I know it sounds severe, but I can't help it. I could be anywhere – walking in the woods, travelling in the car, or even taking a shower – and my inner lawyer[31] will get to work, carefully constructing my case. I'll then rehearse it over

---

31 The phrase 'inner lawyer' is borrowed from Paul David Tripp, *New Morning Mercies: A Daily Gospel Devotional* (IVP, 2014), devotion dated 15 June; and *Dangerous Calling: The Unique Challenges of Pastoral Ministry* (IVP, 2012), p. 12.

and over again, finely honing my argument. It's persuasive. Convincing. Compelling. Happily, I usually win these little lawsuits – which is fairly easy when you take the roles of prosecutor, judge, and jury.

That inner lawyer is in us all. Even from a young age, we have a strong sense of justice. Regular cries of 'It's not fair' will be heard in most households as siblings struggle to get on.

There are times when we all want justice. We all have a strong – if somewhat warped – sense of what is just. Our inner lawyer will prosecute anyone we believe has acted badly, but they will also find an angle to defend us whenever we have done something wrong.

To put that another way, we want justice when we are victims, but we seek to justify ourselves when we are victimisers.

Even criminals justify themselves. After numerous scam phone calls informing me that my computer had been infected by a terrible data-destroying virus, I asked one of the scammers, 'Why are you doing this?' Once he'd got past trying to pretend that he genuinely wanted to help me, he confessed that his actions were because of British colonialism. The British had stolen from his country and now he was stealing something back.

But it's not just scammers who justify wrong behaviour. It's all of us.

We might justify the less attractive aspects of our personality or character by looking back to our upbringing or something we have experienced. And the past does play a part – but it's not the whole story.

Or perhaps, in the moment, we justify our bad behaviour by saying, 'I was tired' or 'I've had a bad day' or 'I just don't know what came over me' – as if, astonishingly, our behaviour even took us by surprise!

In all these ways – and many more – we justify ourselves by effectively claiming that external circumstances conspired against us to make us behave as we did. But rudeness, selfishness, anger, immorality, and the rest only come out of us because they are already in us – as we saw in the last chapter. Our circumstances don't create bad things in us; they merely help to reveal those bad things in us.

It's ironic that we so often try to justify what is blatantly wrong because the word 'justify' is really a word from the courtroom.

To be justified means to be declared innocent, leading to acquittal. No wonder we all want to feel justified!

We will therefore often justify ourselves by trying to be good – perhaps by keeping what we perceive to be the 'rules'. We try to be kind to our neighbour; we let the kids win (sometimes); we carefully categorise our recycling and put it in the right bin or try not to waste energy; if you're British, you definitely don't push in when there's a queue. Many people will feel justified by being politically correct – which is basically keeping a whole set of social rules by doing, saying, and thinking the 'right' thing.

This desire to feel justified is perhaps also why, globally, religion of all kinds is so popular. Generally, all religions work in a similar way: they tell us what we must do (laws to observe, rules to keep, and good deeds to undertake) in order to be acceptable to 'God', or simply acceptable to ourselves. We hope that as a result we will be deemed good enough – justified.

But the wretched thing about it – all of it – is that we never really know if we have done enough … or done it properly. In our worst moments, we know we haven't.

There's no assurance. No certainty. No peace. Doubts linger.

A number of Muslim friends have shared with me how they can never be sure that they will be acceptable to Allah when they are judged. Although they do their best to live according to the Five Pillars of Islam, they are aware of the countless times they have failed. And that means that they really can't be sure if, in the end, they will make the grade. They fear not making it. They have no real peace.

Christianity is very, very different. Wonderfully different! It is not some Western version of Islam or Hinduism or Judaism. It's not another set of rules or laws or principles to observe in order to earn favour with God. It is all about being fully justified without having to rely in any way on our own sketchy and dubious efforts. We are counted by the living God as being completely innocent and perfectly right with Him.

Doesn't that sound good? It is! It's truly wonderful! And better still, this justification is freely available to us all.

You may be thinking, 'But what about obeying the Ten Commandments – aren't they

the laws or rules that Christians have to keep?'
Sure, Christians take God's commandments and
laws seriously – but not in an attempt to earn
His favour. The purpose of God's law was never
a matter of, 'Do these things, and you'll be okay.'
No, the commandments were given to reveal
and reflect what God is like – His perfect and
loving character. 'Do not murder' because God
is a life-giving God. 'Do not commit adultery'
because God is utterly faithful in every way. 'Do
not steal' because God is a generous and giving
God. 'Do not give false witness' because God is
a God of absolute truth.

God's law tells us what God is like, but as it
does so, it makes us conscious that we are not
like that.[32] However hard we may try, we don't
always tell the truth; we are not always faithful;
we are far from God in so many ways.

Trying to keep God's law will not justify us –
it will not allow us to be declared innocent and
right with God – but it was never meant to do
that! As one person helpfully put it, 'The law was
not designed to make us clean. It simply defines

---

32 Romans 3:20.

what clean is!'[33] And then, having shown us by God's standard that we are most certainly not 'clean', it points and leads us to Jesus Christ – the Saviour – so that we may be justified through faith in Him.[34]

Christians are not right with God by observing the commandments or religious laws, but *only by faith in Jesus*.

Without Jesus, God's law would easily and rightly condemn us. There's no point in employing our inner lawyer here. No argument will cut it with God. We are all guilty of not perfectly keeping His law.

And yet God knew we couldn't and wouldn't keep His law. Therefore, out of His huge love for us, He sent His Son, Jesus, to make it possible for us to be truly and fully and properly and completely justified. We are justified not by keeping the law ourselves, but by faith in Jesus who perfectly kept God's law *for us*!

... a person is not justified by the works of the law, but by faith in Jesus Christ. So we, too,

33 Isaac Khalil, 'The Law – A Reflection of God's Character' (lifehopeandtruth.com, article dated 7 January 2015).

34 Galatians 3:24.

*have put our faith in Christ Jesus that we may
be justified by faith in Christ and not by the
works of the law, because by the works of the
law no one will be justified (Galatians 2:16).*

Trying to be justified by keeping any set of rules
(Jewish, Islamic, Christian, Masonic, or personal)
does not work. We cannot be declared innocent
before the living God by any good deeds or law
keeping of our own. For all the good things we
do, there will be as many things – probably more
– which are not good.

Personally, I can't even meet my own lowly
standards, let alone God's perfect standards.
But I can be freely justified by faith in Jesus
Christ – because of what God graciously did
through Him:

*But now apart from the law the righteousness
of God has been made known ... This
righteousness is given through faith in
Jesus Christ to all who believe ... for all
have sinned and fall short of the glory of
God, and all are justified freely by his grace
through the redemption that came by Christ
Jesus. God presented Christ as a sacrifice of*

atonement, through the shedding of his blood
(Romans 3:21–25).

Those beautiful, liberating words tell us that when we put our faith in Jesus, all the nonsensical attempts at self-justification can stop! We have all messed up and fallen far short of God's standards, but redemption is available through Jesus. We can be justified freely by His grace.

God's grace is Him giving us something good that we do not deserve. We do not deserve justification; we actually deserve condemnation. But because of Jesus' sacrifice for all our sin, God is willing to freely justify us. No cost. No conditions. No rules to keep. No laws to observe. No worrying about whether we've made the grade or not. No uncertainty. Jesus has done it all for us.

Do you see that Christianity is not about what we must do for God? It is about what He has kindly done for us!

Jesus perfectly kept God's law. And so when a person believes in Him, God graciously credits Jesus' perfect record to them. They are suddenly and instantly justified! Declared innocent! Fully acquitted!

That's why Christians love and trust Jesus. He has done for us what we could never do for ourselves. The result is peace with God:

> *Therefore, since we have been justified through faith, we have peace with God through our Lord Jesus Christ (Romans 5:1).*

It is this amazing grace and kindness of God that teaches Christians to live as God wants[35] – not out of a duty to keep His law, but as a response to the beauty of His grace. Laws can't change the human heart, but God's grace and goodness to us can. It transforms us!

Furthermore, when we are justified through faith in Jesus, the verdict is secure. It can never be appealed because it is God who justifies us.[36] There is no higher court or judge that could overturn His verdict. The verdict is safe, and so are we. We are safe from ever facing God's judgement!

I want justice. I imagine you do too. But what we *need* is grace. As we have seen throughout

---

35 Titus 2:11–14.
36 Romans 8:33.

this book, we are all guilty: guilty of delusions of independence and self-sufficiency; guilty of idolatrously worshipping created things instead of our Creator; guilty of things for which we are rightly ashamed; guilty of not fully keeping any law – let alone God's law. And guilt leads to shame, feeling lousy, and, ultimately, condemnation. Not even my inner lawyer can justify me. And your inner lawyer can't justify you. But through Jesus, God can.

QUESTIONS TO THINK ABOUT OR DISCUSS

1. When I mess up, do I think it is possible to be justified (declared innocent)? If so, how? What do I think justifies me?

2. What do I do with my guilt? Bury it? Eventually forget about it? Try to atone for it? Something else? Or nothing?

3. What is my response to the grace of God that makes it possible for me to be truly, fully, freely justified by faith in Christ Jesus?

13.

THE INVITATION
TO US ALL

It was a lovely wedding. Then there was the usual photograph rigmarole, which lasted almost as long as the service. Finally, it was time to move into the huge marquee for the banquet reception. I wasn't invited to that part. My friend milked the fact that he was.

Once he'd finished his banter with the 'C-list' (church only) guests, my friend decided to consult the table plan just outside the marquee to find out where, and with whom, he would be sitting. For the length of time he stood there, he must have read each of the two hundred names on that list twice through! He stepped back with a puzzled and slightly disconcerted look. Perhaps he'd missed it? Undeterred, he studied the list again. Nope, his name still wasn't there. Then the banter really began!

One of the hardest things about planning a wedding is working out who to invite. It is often impossible to invite everyone you would like – either the venue or the budget (or both) just can't stretch.

Let me tell you about another wedding – one that we're all invited to as 'A-list' guests. Did you even know that God is planning a wedding? He is. And, wonderfully, God is not limited by space or budget. In fact, He has published an open invitation to us all.

Surprised? In many ways, we should be. We've seen in previous chapters how we ignore God and fail spectacularly in lots of ways, and yet God invites us to His awesome wedding party!

Sadly, most people ignore God's invitation. That's something else that many have in common. But how we respond to God is important – eternally important. Jesus kindly, compassionately, and lovingly warned us that there will be a huge crowd in hell. I don't want to be in that crowd. I don't suppose you do either? We don't have to be!

God has graciously provided a way for us to avoid what we deserve. Instead, we can become part of His family and be at His party. He enabled this through His Son, Jesus.

Jesus did the most loving thing anyone has ever done. It is actually held up as the model for all husbands:

> Husbands, love your wives, just as Christ loved the church and gave himself up for her (Ephesians 5:25).

In the Bible, Jesus is the ultimate loving groom and husband. His bride is the church – that is, everyone who will believe in Him, and love Him, and trust Him. Jesus loved His bride so much that He 'gave himself up for her' as much as is possible: He gave His life; He died. He did this because it was only by His death that His bride could be saved and redeemed from a dead-end way of life that leads to hell. He loves her very much indeed!

The term 'redemption' is to do with paying a price to release someone or something. If my car were towed away because I had parked illegally, I would have to pay the set price to redeem it from wherever it has been impounded.

That's what Jesus did for all who believe and trust in Him. His death paid the full penalty for our sin, so that we may be set free. He paid the necessary price to buy us back and set us free from our delusion, our addictions, our misplaced worship, and our foolish idolatry. He sacrificially gave Himself up to give us life – eternal life in God's family.

And still today Jesus is lovingly pursuing us – He wants us personally to know His deep love and compassion. Maybe, as you have read these pages, you have begun to see how much He loves *you*.

A Christian is someone who sees this astonishing love, sacrifice, and redemption, and humbly says, 'Thank you'. They accept Jesus' free gifts of forgiveness and new life in God's family.

I said earlier that God is planning a wedding and we're invited. But we're not just invited as 'A-list' guests. It's better than that: Jesus is the groom, and He proposes that we be His bride! (Guys, get over it – it's just an image!) What's important is to make sure you understand the image. It tells us that Jesus loves us more deeply and more fully and more passionately than anyone has ever loved us – seen in the way He gave Himself up for us. He is the ultimate groom and He invites us to be His bride.

One of the lovely things about being married is that you get to share everything. On our wedding day, Sharon and I made a number of promises, including, 'All that I have I share with you.' From that day on, whatever either of us had on our own, we now had in common. Sharon got to share my coke bottle collection and my motorbike – lucky girl! I got to share her boy-band music collection and her student debt. Look, I was in love! Still am.

When we accept Jesus' proposal, we haven't anything to share with Him – except the debt of our sin, which He gladly pays by His death. But He has plenty to share with us – things that, from the moment we believe and trust in Him, we will have in common with Him.

Jesus is righteous. And when we believe and trust in Him, God counts us as righteous too.[37]

---

37 Romans 3:22.

Jesus is risen from the grave. And, wonderfully, He shares His resurrection with us. Through Him, we too have the promise of eternal resurrection life.[38] Only He is able to satisfy our desire for life.

Jesus is the Son of God. When we put our faith in Him, God adopts us into His family. He is our loving heavenly Father and we are His children.[39] It's a new identity: we become a child of the living God! Like Jesus, we can call God 'Father'. His image will be gradually renewed in us.[40]

Jesus is now with His Father. Through Jesus, we are reconciled to God.[41] We are no longer distant refugees, but in a loving relationship with Him – such that we may approach Him with confidence.[42] We do not need to approach Him with fear.

We may have many things in common with one another, but it is much, much better to have

---

38 1 Corinthians 15:52; 2 Corinthians 4:14.

39 Romans 8:15; Galatians 4:6; Ephesians 1:5.

40 Colossians 3:10.

41 Romans 5:10.

42 Hebrews 4:16; 10:19.

things in common with Jesus! It is better by a trillion billion miles – and then some!

Of course, all invitations and proposals need a response. So what do you say?

Jesus once told a story about people who were invited to a king's banquet.[43] Sadly, they all gave excuses as to why they could not attend. One had bought a field that he wanted to inspect; another had just purchased some oxen that he wanted to test-drive; and another had just got married, so had his mind on other things!

Their responses were just excuses. The truth is they didn't really want the king. And so they missed out on the wonderful party he had prepared for them.

It's easy to make excuses for refusing King Jesus' invitation and proposal: 'I'm too busy' or 'I haven't time' or 'I have too many questions'. But making excuses is ultimately inexcusable. And it will mean missing out.

My friend's name was not on the wedding-party guest list, so he missed out, and was disappointed.

---

43 Luke 14:16–23.

The final book of the Bible describes the end of time when God will judge us all by consulting His guest list and seeing who has accepted His invitation:

> And I saw the dead, great and small, standing before the throne, and books were opened. Another book was opened, which is the book of life ... Anyone whose name was not found written in the book of life was thrown into the lake of fire (Revelation 20:12, 15).

These are very sobering words. This is the one guest list from which we don't want to be missing.

There can be no banter about not being on it, for the 'lake of fire' is a terrifying picture of hell – of eternal separation from God and from all the good things He has in store for those who love and trust Him.

But God has given this sobering image to warn us and to move us – because He loves us so much.

Instead of just having things in common with every human being, why not accept the invitation to have eternally significant and glorious things in common with Jesus? He really does love you so much that He gave Himself up for you.

Our response could be a bit like how I shop. Sometimes I see something I want, but then go away and think about it – either to make sure that I really need or want it, or to do a bit more research. Other times I will see something in a shop – even something that I wasn't really looking for – and instantly know that it is a *really* good thing and that I 'need' it. So I'll get it there and then.

Perhaps you'd like to go away and think about God's invitation. That's a great thing to do. If what you have read in this book is true – and it is – then there is nothing more important to think about. We often say, 'It's good to have an open mind.' At some point, though, having weighed the evidence and information, it's also good to be able to close our mind on the truth – to make our decision.

Others will want to do some more research and ask some questions. If a Christian gave you this book, perhaps they could answer your questions. Or you could find a church that will help you (see my suggestions in the postscript). Ask away with all the questions that you have!

The truth will withstand any amount of probing – that's what makes it the truth.

But it may be that as you have read this book, you have been persuaded. You know that what you have seen about yourself (and, indeed, all of us) is true. You have seen how Jesus is both good and God – someone we *really* need if we are to be saved from ourselves, saved from our sin, saved for God, and saved for eternal life. And so you already know that you would like to believe and trust in Him. You want to accept God's invitation, through Jesus, to join His family. If that's you, then you can do that even right now.

Prayer is simply talking to God. You don't need special language or phrases. Just talk to God in your own words about your response to all that you have read. You might want to somehow express your sorrow at your sin; your thankfulness for Jesus; your desire, from now on, to believe in Him as your personal King and Saviour; and your longing to be part of God's family. The words themselves are not the most important thing – God knows what is going on in your heart, and will welcome you regardless of how eloquent or garbled your words are. But if you want an example of what you might say, the prayer below is something a person could pray if they wanted to accept God's offer and become a Christian.

Heavenly Father, I acknowledge today that I have worshipped created things instead of you, my Creator.

I have been deluded about my own goodness. I have wandered far from you and tried to live independently.

Thank you for Jesus – the Way, the Truth, and the Life. Thank you that, on the cross, He gave Himself up to pay the penalty for my sin. Thank you that He rose from the grave to give me new life.

Today I turn back to you and put my faith in Jesus.

Because of Jesus, please forgive me and change me so that, from this day on, I may live as one of your children and as part of the bride of Christ.

Amen.

POSTSCRIPT

If you have just sincerely prayed the prayer on the previous page (or your own prayer), then today is a wonderful day for you! Praise God many times. You have just moved from slavery to freedom; from darkness to light; from death to life – it really is that significant and big!

As of right now you have the most important things in common with Jesus: you are right with God; you are a much-loved member of His family; and you are an heir, with Jesus, of all that God has promised and prepared for those who love Him.

The Christian life is a life with God – knowing Him and being known by Him. It is enjoying

Him! In the most important sense everything has changed.

But the Christian life is also a life of recovery. All Christians have this in common: we are each in recovery from our former life without God.

Recovery is often slow – so, in another sense, not everything will change straight away. Perhaps that's just as well as, typically, we're not very good at change.

Little by little, though, God will help us to change. He will expose things in our lives that aren't right or good, and gradually reform us into the people He wants us to be – people who instead of worshipping created things, increasingly worship our Creator; who instead of putting faith in ourselves or others, have faith in our loving and faithful heavenly Father; who instead of being deluded, see ourselves rightly and so are dependent on Him for life and breath and every good thing; and who instead of being controlled by anxiety and fear, trust the One who rules over all, knowing that He cares for us.

From the moment you became a Christian, God gave three things to help you:

1. His Holy Spirit – who has just moved in to your life. The Holy Spirit is the Spirit of God. He will help you to understand God's word, to trust Jesus, and to live with Him as your personal Lord and Saviour.

2. His word (the Bible). God gives us His word so that we don't have to guess about Him or about how we should live as His children. The Bible tells us everything we need to know about living as a child of God and as the bride of Christ.

3. His people (the church) to encourage and spur us on in our Christian life. We need one another to keep going!

It's worth knowing that not all churches are the same. The denomination (or type) is not especially important, but try to find a local church that seeks to clearly and faithfully teach God's word. It should have the aim of helping people to come to know Jesus and then to live for Him each day. Also look out for a fellowship of people who love and care for each other – people who are involved in one another's lives, and who intentionally seek to encourage each other in their faith and in actively following Jesus in ordinary life.

You may find a good church near you on one of these sites:

WORLDWIDE

- The Gospel Coalition –
  www.thegospelcoalition.org/churches/

- Acts 29 Network –
  www.acts29.com/find-a-church/

- International Presbyterian Church (IPC) –
  https://ipc.church

IN AMERICA

- The Gospel Coalition –
  www.thegospelcoalition.org/churches/

- Acts 29 Network –
  www.acts29.com/find-a-church/

- Presbyterian Church in America (PCA) –
  https://pcanet.org

IN EUROPE

- The Gospel Coalition –
  www.thegospelcoalition.org/churches/

- Acts 29 Network –
  www.acts29.com/network/europe/

- Fellowship of Independent Evangelical
  Churches (FIEC) –
  www.fiec.org.uk/churches

- Evangelical Alliance – www.eauk.org

- Anglican Mission in England (AMiE) –
  www.anglicanmissioninengland.org/our-
  churches/

- International Presbyterian Church (IPC) –
  https://ipc.church

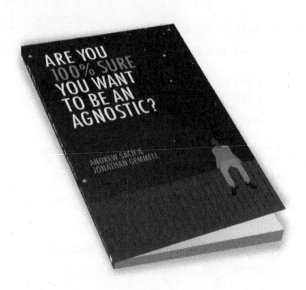

ARE YOU
100% SURE
YOU WANT
TO BE AN
AGNOSTIC?

ANDREW SACH &
JONATHAN GEMMELL

10 Publishing